D0188131

The
Executive
Writer

**A Guide to Managing Words,
Ideas, and People**

Edith Poor

Montemayor Press

Millburn, New Jersey

For information address:
Montemayor Press,
P. O. Box 526, Millburn, NJ 07041
Web site: MontemayorPress.com

First Montemayor Press Edition 2008

1 3 5 7 9 10 8 6 4 2

Library of Congress Cataloging-in-Publication Data

Poor, Edith.
  The executive writer: a guide to managing words, ideas, and people / Edith Poor.
     p. cm.
  ISBN 0-8021-3290-1 (pbk.)
1. Communication in management. 2. Business writing
I. Title.
HD30.3.P66   1992   91-18075
808'.066658—cd20   CIP

About Edith Poor

Edith Poor helps business leaders think, write, and speak more clearly. She has over twenty years' experience helping executives master the printed and spoken word.

Her clients include leaders in consulting, higher education, financial services, computer technology, telecommunications, and health care. As a former communications specialist for Booz Allen & Hamilton—a leading international management consulting firm—she spent five years traveling throughout the U.S., Europe, and the Far East, helping executives communicate better.

Edith Poor began her career in the publishing industry, where she developed, edited, marketed, and promoted best-selling books on everything from economics to ethnomusicology. She was an editor at Charles Scribner's Sons Publishers for five years. She earned a B.A. with honors from Smith College, Northampton, Massachusetts. She has done research in speech and language at Leeds University in England, and is a former member of the adjunct faculty at New York University's Stern School of Business Administration.

In addition to *The Executive Writer*, she has written *Voicework: Women, Men, and Public Speaking* (Montemayor Press, 2001), which examines the "masculine" style of public speaking prevalent in the corporate world. She is at work on a book about communication and leadership.

Contact information

Web: www.edithpoor.com
E-mail: edithpoor@edithpoor.com

To E. J. M.—
and for his example

Acknowledgments

What a conventional place for what seems to me such unconventional thanks.

First thanks to my husband, Ed Myers, whose skill as a writer is surpassed only by his generosity as an editor.

Thanks to John Wright, my agent, for his advocacy throughout. Editors Bill Strachan and Joy Johannessen saw early drafts of the book and believed in it. Jim Moser edited the final version with skill, insight, and tact. I'm grateful for Susan Tillack's able assistance throughout, the scrupulous copyediting of Anna Jardine, and Chris Potash's painstaking work on the proofs.

Thanks to a host of supporters and readers: Robin Myers, Josephine Diagonale, William Zinsser, Delia Marshall, Randy Jacob, Ann Thibodeau, Andrew Lynch, Susan Poor, Geoff Poor, Roger Poor, Henry Poor, Erik Anderson, Jane Blatt, Mike Blatt, Caroline Hanly, Kate Carty, Joe Reilly, Katrin Stroh, and Tony Townsend.

And my thanks to colleagues and clients, many of whom helped, I suspect, without realizing it: Joanna Cole, Judy Esterquest, Ruth Danon, Paul Hunter, Chris Kelly, Cille Koch, David Young, Bob Sherlock, Susan Beauregard, Doreen Kryzsik, Bill Perry, Dorrie Kelly, Jack Wright, and Mike Siegel.

Contents

Introduction   xi

CHAPTER ONE
Management by Writing   3
The way you write is a telling snapshot of the way
you manage.

CHAPTER TWO
Words Written, Words Read:
A Management Parable   19
The writer must manage the reader.

CHAPTER THREE
The Management of Thinking   35
An aerial view of the writing task will make the
whole process more efficient.

CHAPTER FOUR
Negotiating with the Reader   53
Your writing is the answer to a question. There are
only three that matter: What? Why? How?

CHAPTER FIVE

Using Space, Using Silence 75

*The way to the reader's mind is through the eye
and ear.*

CHAPTER SIX

Editing: The Politics 105

The challenge: keeping the writer's ego intact.

CHAPTER SEVEN

Editing: The Tools 127

The challenge: keeping the writer's meaning intact.

Conclusion 137

Sources 139

Introduction

This book is about writing in the corporate world. It's for managers and executives who find themselves spending too much time writing when they could be managing.

I don't propose to show you how to speed-write so you'll have time to get back to what really matters—managing. I do propose, however, to show you how to use writing to *help* you manage. Writing is part of your job, after all; but it's also a dimension of your management style, one that few managers fully exploit.

Writing is a management task and in some ways a management chore. But if that is the only way you think of writing, you will never be able to use it as a management tool. This book treats writing as a management tool and shows you how to use it.

The conventional wisdom about business writing can be summed up in four tips—tips you already know.

1. Get to the point.
2. Tell them what you're going to tell them, then tell them, then tell them what you just told them.
3. Use short sentences.
4. Avoid the passive voice.

This is the formula. The result? Simple documents, simply written. But my question is this: If you follow the formula, will you be an effective communicator?

Don't misunderstand me—clarity and brevity are important building blocks of effective communication; it's just that they're not ends in themselves. You don't write to be brief and clear; you write briefly and clearly to motivate your staff, get the promotion, convince senior management to approve the budget. There's another dimension to business writing, one that goes beyond the building blocks of brevity and clarity. And that is the management dimension.

In the corporate world, writing involves far more than getting your ideas down on paper. It involves negotiating the movement of those ideas through the organization so that people will act on them.

You need to think clearly about your document from the reader's perspective as well as your own. You need to assess—and exploit—the political climate in your organization or department. You need to structure your ideas so that they affect the reader as much as they've affected you.

In other words, you need to think about a lot more than the length of your sentences. You need a strategic focus, not just a tactical one.

The management dimension of writing has as much to do with the process of writing as with the product. Corporations are group settings in which multiple writers are often involved in the same task. To manage that task well, we must jettison what I call the "myth of authorship": that beguiling illusion that every writer can think, and achieve, in creative solitude. In business the reality is different. More often than not, writing is a clamorous, inefficient, highly political group effort for which recognition is rarely given. It's a skilled manager indeed who can guide the process—and develop the people at the same time.

The Executive Writer is the product of the more than ten years I've spent as a communications consultant to senior management. My typical clients are recently promoted executives confronting a dizzying array of communications tasks for which they feel ill prepared. These tasks involve both writing and public speaking; it's rare that one doesn't lead naturally to the other. In corporate life, writing and speaking are two sides of the same managerial coin, and it makes sense to treat them that way.

My clients have much in common. They are blessed with intelligence, tenacity, ambition, and a sense of irony. And they realize that their communications skills are getting in the way instead of helping to pave it.

I have written *The Executive Writer* with such people in mind: the newly promoted vice-president of a computer technology firm, the chief financial officer of a large bank, the national marketing director of a manufacturing concern, the personnel director of a financial services firm. All of them see writing as the enemy, a sentence (no pun intended) they have to serve. They hire me to show them how to use writing as an enabling rather than a constraining force in their lives.

Few people expect me to show them how to *like* writing, but often this is precisely what happens. It happens because liking it comes with feeling that you've taken charge: you've harnessed the writing process to serve you, your goals, and your objectives. Inevitably, taking charge of writing means taking charge, period; it means managing. Managing yourself as thinker and doer, and managing the thinking and doing of others. For many that process is exhilarating.

Why? Because the ability to communicate is power itself. Indeed, the ability to communicate is management itself. Words motivate. They demoralize. They incite, they placate, they appease. They wound. They heal. They *matter*.

I deplore the five-step method to thinking, to writing, to managing. (This book will not sit comfortably next to *The One-Minute Anything*.) But the business world requires that communicators synthesize and present intricate, subtle ideas simply. So for the record, here is what I believe:

Writing is not the hard part; thinking is. Thinking is so hard that we probably invented writing to make thinking easier.

The way an organization writes reveals much about how it thinks. The way *you* write reveals much about how *you* think. Improve the writing and inevitably you improve the quality of the thinking.

Writing is managing. Managing requires the ability to listen to those around you. Writing requires the ability to "listen" to the reader. How? You must learn to anticipate the reader's responses—document by document, paragraph by paragraph, sentence by sentence—and plan for them. You must manage the reader's expectations.

The Executive Writer treats writing as a management tool. It analyzes the pressures of corporate life. It shows how to speak for your facts and your convictions with the authority and the coherence that your position requires. It illustrates how to develop your staff by showing them how to do what you do: communicate clearly.

THE
EXECUTIVE
WRITER

CHAPTER ONE

Management by Writing

The great battleground in corporate America is neither the boardroom nor the trading floor—it's the printed page. Writers and readers joust there daily. Fortunes rise and fall; reputations bloom and wither. People write, read, and act.

. . .

You are a division vice-president for a computer software firm. The division president has asked you to write a confidential report outlining a strategy for restructuring your division. Needless to say, this recommendation will affect, and alienate, most of your colleagues. You feel tortured, disloyal, pressured—and cannot seem to get started.

. . .

You were hired from another bank one year ago. You were promoted to vice-president six months ago. It's time for your first appraisal. Your boss is too busy to do the necessary paperwork. She says, "You write the performance review and then we'll go over it." Salary increases are directly related to this document. You know that your boss is the most unassuming person on the planet, and she hates people who grandstand. You have one day to write the appraisal.

•   •   •

You have just hired a new secretary. You tell her to handle all your correspondence. She has been on the job three days; you have spent exactly half an hour with her. You've given her examples to follow, but none of her drafts comes out right. You're irritated. So is she.

•   •   •

Outlandish scenarios? They're all real. So are these:

•   •   •

You have to write your resignation.

•   •   •

You are a former English teacher and everyone in the department knows it. Your colleagues routinely seek you out for help with their writing. At first you were flattered; now you are merely drained.

•   •   •

You are a highly quantitative manager who reports to the senior vice-president. He does not understand numbers.

•   •   •

You are a highly verbal sort who reports to a manager demanding that everything be explained as a regression analysis.

•   •   •

You are president of the company. You studied Shake-speare as a graduate student at Princeton twenty-five years ago and can recite almost all of Hamlet's "To be or not to be" soliloquy. You have been known to spend an entire morning correcting the grammatical errors in the memos that cross your desk. Your staff is terrified of you.

.　　.　　.

These snapshots of corporate life show people managing, or being managed, by writing—with varying degrees of forethought, efficiency, and success.

Many management behaviors are reflected in the not always crystal-clear pool of your writing style. When I say "writing style," of course, I mean a lot more than the choice and arrangement of words on the page. I mean a whole slew of assumptions, attitudes, fears, habits, and pressures that you drag around the office and onto the page—along with the words.

This behavioral grab-bag is the raw material for a lot more than your writing. It's also the core of your managerial self: the self who interacts with peers, subordinates, and senior management. Writing is a form of management behavior. The way you manage people is reflected in the way you manage words; the way you manage words is a reflection of the way you manage people.

I've spent over a decade helping writers to identify and understand the relationships between writing and managing. As a writing consultant, I work with clients on marketing and sales documents, technical specifications, management proposals, progress reviews, strategic plans, annual reports, speeches, presentations, and articles and books for publication. Inevitably, we focus on more than the document. We talk about the complex web of influences that makes writing and managing so difficult.

Some of those influences spring right from the pressures at hand: an impossible deadline; the spirited meeting next door, every word of it audible; lack of information, and lack of access to those who can supply it. While not earth-shattering, these are the annoyances and petty inconveniences of organizational life. They contribute mightily to the joylessness that most people ascribe to the writing process.

Other influences are more subtle and therefore more insidious. I'm referring here to a shapeless, free-floating anxiety—endemic in corporations throughout the land—about the safety or wisdom of saying what you mean and meaning what you say. Writers suffering from this condition spend an inordinate amount of time and energy speculating tensely about the political consequences of what they write. *How will this document affect my job, promotion, raise, reputation, or future?*

To write in a corporate environment is to expose yourself to the politics of that environment, and to risk involvement in ways you don't want and never intended. It would be a mistake, however, to think that the fear of political fallout can't be addressed and even overcome. Political sensitivity is essential to good writing. There isn't a writing task worth doing that doesn't contain some risk for the writer, the reader, or both. I'll return to this issue frequently; it's at the core of what makes writing so hard and so rewarding.

There's another influence at work too, and it's the most elusive and pervasive of them all. Beneath the anxieties about deadlines and politics lies the fear of writing itself. By this I mean anxiety about the actual process of writing: its open-endedness; its inefficiency; its laboriousness. Uncertainty about how to begin, how to end. Confusion about what the reader expects. A deeply held sense that the final product won't be much good, and the absolute certainty that the process of getting there will be painful.

"What do you think of your writing?" I ask this question of all my clients. The responses are all over the map in their particulars: too long; too short; too wordy; too boring; too time-consuming. But there's a general theme that runs throughout: an unease, an insecurity, an anxiousness. For almost everybody—even those who say they enjoy it—the writing process evokes feelings of dread and inadequacy.

Let's face it. The way you manage words has a lot to do with the way you and your words were managed when you were a student. The way you write reflects the way you were taught to write, and the way you were edited. (Notice that I make no mention of being taught *how* to edit. No one is taught how to edit. It's supposed to be obvious . . . like managing.)

When I first work with a client, I make a point of asking, "When you think back to how you were taught to write, what do you remember? What seems most vivid?" Responses typically fall into three categories:

1. I remember nothing. I wasn't taught to write.
   No one can teach anyone how to write, anyway.
2. I had a wonderful teacher in the seventh

[fourth, eleventh] grade who taught me everything I know. That class changed my life.
3. Diagramming sentences. That's what I remember.

To those in category 1, who believe that writing can't
be taught, I say (echoing veteran journalist and writing
teacher William Zinsser): You're right. Writing can't be
taught. But it can be learned.

To those in category 2, who feel the permanent, positive imprint of a literary mentor, I point out the essential
humanity of that relationship and say: You were indeed
fortunate, and you still are.

To those in category 3, who remember only those
scaffolds from which they had to hang limp, dismem-
bered sentences from their textbooks, I say: No wonder
you hate to write.

Why are so many writers so unsure of themselves?
Why is it that even those who communicate well are so
quick to deride their weaknesses, dismiss their abilities,
and deny their potential? Why do we feel insecurity as
writers? What is the source of this insecurity?

Sister Mary had a lot to do with it. One of my clients,
reminiscing about her early writing education, said:

What I remember most, from all those years of diagramming sentences and writing book reports, is what I call
the Grammar God. Sister Mary had a direct line to the
Grammar God, and she warned us of the sins of the split
infinitive, the dangling modifier, the abuses of the semi-
colon. I was petrified of her.

The company president who edits compulsively and terrorizes his* staff—he still considers himself a sinner, and he continues to atone. I am certain of it. And he is not alone. I am struck by how many people had a Grammar God to appease as they grew up. (Incidentally, writers who look back today often do so gratefully. The lessons stuck. It's not clear how many of today's fifth-graders will be able, twenty years hence, to recall their instruction so vividly.)

But how did Sister Mary manage it? How is it that these eternal truths about language became so firmly imprinted in an entire generation of schoolchildren? What is their impact on us as adult writers, readers, and managers?

Our writing teachers offered us the promise of certainty in an uncertain world. Indeed, they delivered on that promise. How reassuring it was (and is) to be able to say: The first word in every sentence *must always* begin with a capital letter. The subject and verb *must always* agree. You *must never* use a split infinitive.

The line between certainty and uncertainty is a hard one to draw where writing is concerned. Some of the rules are cast in stone; some are written in sand and are gradually eroded by new patterns of thought and usage. But which are which?

Many adult writers hold tenaciously to every rule they can remember, regardless of how appropriate it is to their current patterns of thought and usage. Such tenacity can backfire, and it has done so for much of corporate America. Let me give just one example.

---

* In this book I use the generic pronoun "he."

"Never use the personal pronoun 'I' when you write," Sister Mary would say. "It's wrong to draw attention to yourself."

I know what she was getting at. I know what she was trying to prevent:

> I think this is a good book. I think that the reason that Jack and Jake were carried off by the pirate was because he wasn't really a pirate—I think he was really their father, only they hadn't seen him for so long that I don't think they recognized him. I think that he was really trying to save them from Mr. Bailey. I think that Mr. Bailey was the real pirate, only I think that he was disguised as the lawyer who was supposed to take care of their money until they were old enough to have it themselves, but I think he was going to try to steal the money by pretending to be the lawyer. . . .

I can imagine such a book report. At the top, a blue star and the words: "It's clear that you put a lot of thought into this report. Next time, though, be sure to write without saying 'I think.' The fact that you're writing this means that these are your thoughts. It's not a good idea to draw attention to yourself."

Thirty years later, and our budding communicator has successfully navigated high school and college English ("Is this going to be on the final? . . . What do you want in this paper? . . . How long does it have to be?"). He has a job or two under his belt; perhaps several. In each instance, the writer learns how he is read (how he is graded). This is how.

For all the reasons outlined above, it seems to be prudent to find a solution to the pricing problem as soon as is humanly possible. Also, it is the responsibility of this department to be closely allied with the marketing and the purchasing departments. Together, these three groups should be systematically reviewing all the viable pricing options in order to clearly identify the one set of parameters that is most accurate in terms of the profitability objectives that were established by the planning committee at the last strategy offsite.

The grammatical errors are few and minor (note the split infinitive "to clearly identify" in the third sentence). But thirty years—and countless book reports, term papers, memos, presentations, and final reports—later, that fifth-grade caution against the personal pronoun "I" resonates in the echo chambers of corporate life and letters.

Result: the link between the thinker and his thoughts has been airbrushed out of existence. It's impossible to detect *what* this writer thinks. He has achieved what literary critic George Steiner calls "the immunity of indirection."

And with that achievement comes the loss of his own natural speaking voice—the voice of his thoughts. He has lost the sense of self—personality, style, call it what you will—without which ideas flatten and fail.

It is here, of course, that writing and managing become indistinguishable. Good writing *is* good management. Effective management has no room for flat, voiceless ideas set adrift on the page or in the organization. Effective management is the province not of failed ideas but of successful ones, successfully communicated.

But surely, you say, the presence or absence of the personal pronoun "I" has very little to do with all of this. To which I reply: It's not the physical presence or absence of the pronoun on the page that matters. What matters is the real presence of the "I" in the writer-manager's mind. This "I" links the writer to his ideas, thereby giving him a sense of control, balance, and clarity. It gives the manager the perspective he needs to succeed as the formulator, marketer, and implementer of those ideas. Without this "I" there can be no effective writing and no effective management.

How to inject this sense of "presence" into your writing style and management style? Use your natural speaking voice, the voice of "I" and "we":

> We need to solve the pricing problem immediately. This department will spend the next week working with the marketing and purchasing departments. Our objective: to find the best pricing structure, given the profitability objectives from the last strategy meeting.

Lots of changes here. The first sentence:

> . . . it seems to be prudent [to whom?] to find a solution to the pricing problem as soon as is humanly [as opposed to divinely?] possible . . .

becomes a statement of conviction:

We need to solve the pricing problem immediately. . . .

followed by a projected course of action:

This department will spend the next week working
with the marketing and purchasing departments . . .
to find the best pricing structure . . .

Conviction and action are essential to good management, and they go together. Corporations are full of people with strong beliefs—but without a useful plan of action, those beliefs seldom get very far. By the same token, corporate America bustles with plans, recommendations, initiatives—but what good are they without strong, logical convictions? Good writing demonstrates to your reader that you have both. Good writing keeps you *present*—as a writer and as a manager.

When you sit down to write, you sit down with yourself. Or to be more precise, when you sit down to write, you sit down to find yourself. To find out what you know and what you don't; what you can say and what you can't. When you sit down to write, you sit down to find the words that define your beliefs.

It's impossible to sit down with yourself when you've banned yourself from the room. And yet by banishing the personal pronoun from our writing, that's precisely what we've done. The result: we're not there.

The management parallels are striking. Too often managers are invisible, or they're visible only intermittently. They're often absent when needed most: when conviction and action are called for.

What I'm describing is rudderless management—symbolized by weak, rudderless writing. It's no wonder that we struggle with style; that our writing seems stiff; that our writing is hard to follow; that our writing is boring.

It's no wonder that we hate to write, and find writing a difficult, circuitous process. And no wonder that, as writers, editors, and managers, we tie each other in knots.

I once asked a mathematician when it was that he first got interested in math, and his answer surprised me. "I actually disliked math all the way through school and college. In fact, it wasn't until after I got my Ph.D. that I really began to enjoy it." When I asked him why, he said, "You have to get beyond the numbers. Numbers aren't math. You have to get beyond being graded and judged and fulfilling everyone else's expectations of your proficiency with the numbers. That's when the fun starts."

The same can be said of writing. You have to get beyond the words. Words aren't writing. You have to get beyond being graded and judged and fulfilling everyone else's expectations of your proficiency with the words. That's when the fun starts.

Unfortunately, very few of us turn into mathematicians or writers in this sense. We are stymied by numbers and words and the expectations of those who judge our proficiency at manipulating them.

Those expectations go back a long way, to our early teachers. After all, they (along with our parents) were our first managers, our first mentors. They're with us still: when we write, when we edit, when we manage.

Do you have to be a brilliant writer to be a good manager? No. Do you have to be a good writer to be a good manager? It helps. A lot.

The link between management style and writing style receives precious little attention—particularly at the senior ranks—but it deserves all the light and air you can give it. Why? For two reasons. First, it's a way to get further faster: management by writing increases your visibility and demonstrates leadership.

And while we're on the subject of leadership—you didn't ask to be a role model, but it comes with the turf. Chances are you're wearing many more hats than you ever thought you would. Which brings me to the second reason good writing is so important. Like it or not, you're a writing instructor in your organization, simply because you're a manager. Your staff looks to you, looks at your writing, to see how to get things said so that things get done. There's a great deal riding on your skills as teacher, coach, and mentor.

Given what we know about the workforce of the 1990s, your role as writing instructor is bound to expand. You face an employment pool of unprecedented cultural and educational diversity.

You face a population of young employees whose writing, reading, and even thinking skills are largely undeveloped. They are unprepared for the communications tasks required in any professional environment: collecting information, listening, asking questions, analyzing what's important, summarizing, drawing logical conclusions, making a case. Training departments are responding energetically, but they will not be able to do it all, particularly in lean times. The training will be done by you, and it will be decidedly OJT.

A manager in a large computer services firm said to me recently, "Writing is becoming increasingly easy to avoid in this organization. We do everything by conference call or electronic mail. Everything is international, global. Everything moves fast, and writing is slow." These remarks followed her observations about the generally poor quality of her staff's communication skills.

There's a connection. As a writing and speaking consultant, I see increasing evidence that the ability to communicate is held hostage by the inability to think. When we remove writing from the equation, we often remove clear thinking too. The seductive speed of fax, phone, and electronic mail has blunted the urge to formulate a thoughtful, analytical response. Speed drives substance. Decisions are made, resources allocated, money spent as fast as the electronic impulse strikes.

Writing is a bridge between thought and communication. But speed is here to stay, and the electronic impulse will continue to accelerate the pace at which we must think in order to do business. Good writing is more important now than ever before. My goal, therefore, is to help people write—and think—faster and smarter.

A banking client lamented: "Very few people are rewarded in corporate life for their ability to communicate; you're rewarded only for meeting revenue goals. You're accountable for the numbers, but no one cares how you get them." This is unfortunate. Especially since one of the best ways to get them is to be an effective manager—which means being an effective communicator.

I acknowledge that the corporate voice may be more in control of the page than the writer is. I can't solve the politics. I can't create the kind of environment that will make writing easy. All I can do is point out that writing is woven into the very fabric of organizational life, and that the texture of the cloth is made up of individual writers sitting down to find themselves.

How to be a good writer-manager? Whoever you are, whatever your title and position, do not be deceived by the organization chart. Reporting relationships are not what they seem. They are not, for example, two-dimensional black lines on a page. (Nor, for that matter, are words.) They are human relationships that require human behavior.

A heretical strategy: Be yourself. A heretical tactic: When you write, sound like the human being you are. Put the "I"—or the "we"—back in. The stronger your own voice, the stronger your identity and power as a manager. The stronger your own voice, the stronger the organization's. (Strangely, this does not work in reverse. Food for thought.)

CHAPTER TWO

Words Written, Words Read: A Management Parable

> You write. You push a pencil across the page, or tap a keyboard and follow the blinking cursor on the screen. You do a couple of drafts, maybe several—and then you hand the document over to an assistant, who cleans it up, prints it, and sends it out. End of story.

We're born. We scream and then babble; we make sounds. We make sounds that make sense. Producing the appropriate noises, we make words. We use what we hear; we invent our own; we ape and mimic the words of others.

We're card-carrying conversationalists by then (we're public speakers—as any speaker automatically becomes). Chances are we're crayon-carrying conversationalists too—which means that we're burgeoning writers. Before we know it, we've learned the alphabet. Next thing we know, we have a memo to write, or a final report, or a speech.

In this small way each of us encapsulates the entire history of communication. Ontology recapitulates phylogeny. (Remember that from high-school biology?) In each of us, and in our growth and development as communicators, is played out the intricate, tangled relationship between speaking and writing for the whole of the human species.

That relationship goes back thousands of years—no one knows precisely how many. But its legacy remains, and we would be better writers if we understood it more than we do.

Writing needs always to be aware of its honest, humble roots in human speech.* Speech came first. Speech is old; writing is newer. Speech is personal, organic: it comes from inside us, from our bodies. We use nerves and muscles to produce it. Writing, by contrast, is impersonal, mechanical, even technological: it requires a tool, an implement.

Speech unites. Speaker and listener are face to face, engaged in a give-and-take that occurs in real time. (Hence the power of a gifted speaker.)

Writing, by contrast, separates. It separates us from our speech and thus from ourselves.

But most important, writing separates us from each other. The development of writing meant that speech no longer had to happen in real time. Writing, in essence, freeze-dried human speech so that the "listener" could "hear" it later.

The benefits of this development are incalculable, to be sure. But so are the pitfalls. One seems to me especially pernicious:

---

* My remarks about the relationship between writing and speech are heavily influenced by Walter J. Ong's provocative book *Orality & Literacy: The Technologizing of the Word* (New York and London: Methuen, 1982).

It's hard to talk to someone who isn't there.

You feel awkward. You stare at the page and think about what to say, how to start, how to *sound.* When preparing a speech or presentation you experience a comparable unease; when you rehearse out loud, the whole process is artificial, because there's no one there to hear remarks that you're uttering precisely *to be heard.*

And so the dilemma: How can you talk to someone who isn't there? How can you engage in a give-and-take when there's no one there to do the taking?

The writer, of course, must imagine the taking: he must imagine the reader. The reader must do his part: he must imagine the writer. Each must simulate a dialogue, a conversation, with the other.

Writing is dialogue imagined. But conversations are tricky things, and the imagination is fickle and inconsistent. Unless you're very careful, you're going to end up talking not to your reader but to yourself.

Monologues have no place in business writing or in management, but they're abundant. Here's one example—an ordinary business memo written in haste. I'm going to tackle it from two angles in this chapter—the writer's and the reader's. Only by examining both perspectives will we be able to put our finger on why writing, reading, and managing are so difficult.

Monologue, Not Dialogue: Writer Converses with Self

Date: May 6
To: Bob Hartwig
From: Carla Mendez
Subject: May 2 Meeting

This memo is in response to some questions from last Friday's meeting.

At the conference we need 100 blank manila envelopes, the preprinted material, a sample registration form, and reply cards. We'll also need 75 manila envelopes containing preprinted materials, plus 100 evaluation sheets.

Preconference materials need to be mailed by May 30. Envelopes for this mailing should be the ones with the new design as approved. Preconference material packet includes: preprinted materials, sample registration forms, and reply cards/evaluation sheets.

Address on mailing envelopes: Sarah will let you know which. Reply cards must fit into mailing envelopes.

Still to come: preconference material, a decision on return address, reply cards, and the conference agenda (we should have about 200 of these at the conference registration table).

It's important that we take Ezra's concerns about price very seriously. As I mentioned, our phone conversation last week underscored how important his input is.

This should wrap it up. I'm sure you can handle

everything from here on. I'm leaving tomorrow for a three-week tour of our Asian subsidiaries, followed by some vacation time. See you at the conference.

Try an experiment. Take this memo. Write each sentence on a separate index card and shuffle the pack. Hand the batch to four people and ask each to come up with the best sequence.

You'll get four different memos—five if you count the original. And the original may or may not be the best of the lot.

Reading is an interpretive act. It's an interpretive act under the best of circumstances (which this experiment clearly isn't). Under the worst it's a wild goose chase.

Why? Because writing and reading are opposites. They're mirror images of each other.

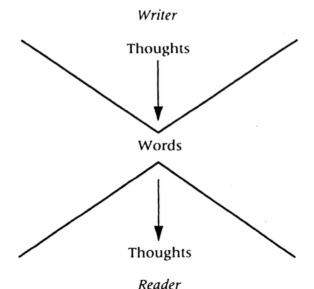

Writer

Thoughts

Words

Thoughts

Reader

In writing this paragraph, for example, my job is to transform my thoughts into words. In reading this paragraph, your job is to transform my words into thoughts. Words and thoughts are not the same thing. We use one to capture the other; rarely, if ever, are we completely successful.

The writer of this memo, Carla Mendez, is writing to get it all down. Writing it down as it spins around in her head. Writing selectively, subjectively, and under pressure—before she leaves for three weeks in Asia. She expects the conference to fall into place during that time, on the basis of the instructions in this memo. She *needs* it to fall into place.

She is writing not so much to Bob Hartwig as to herself: This needs to get done, and also this, and this needs to get taken care of, and don't forget this and this. The only "dialogue" at work here is Carla's impatient racking of her own brain: What else? What else? What else?

In evaluating such a piece of writing, I apply the so-called Act-of-God writing test. Your reader (in this case Bob Hartwig) gets hit by a tornado or a Mack truck or a bad back; how easily can his replacement figure out what needs to be done? (You, of course, are at that moment clearing customs in Hong Kong.)

Faced with a document that is little more than the writer's interior monologue, the reader falls back on an interior monologue of his own. The manager uses the page to think out loud, thereby failing to communicate clearly. The employee spends time and energy figuring out his boss and his message—time that should be spent doing what's being asked. To put it simply, the job isn't getting done.

So we have the all too common situation at the heart of human communication: speaker and listener, writer and reader, worlds apart, muttering away.

Here's the memo again, annotated to give the reader his say:

Monologue, Not Dialogue: Reader Converses with Self

Writer	*Reader*
This memo is in response to some questions from last Friday's meeting.	What questions?
At the conference we need 100 blank manila envelopes, the preprinted material, a sample registration form, and reply cards.	Does all this stuff get put in the manila envelopes or what? What's this preprinted material? Why only one sample registration form—or is that one per envelope?
We'll also need 75 manila envelopes containing preprinted materials, plus 100 evaluation sheets.	So we need 100 blank manila envelopes in all, right? Do they contain anything besides the preprinted materials? What are these evaluation sheets?

Writer	*Reader*
Preconference materials need to be mailed by May 30. Envelopes for this mailing should be the ones with the new design as approved.	Now wait a minute . . . are these the same envelopes as the blank manila ones? How can they be blank if they have this new design? And what do you mean, "as approved"?
Preconference material packet includes: preprinted materials, sample registration forms, and reply cards/evaluation sheets.	I thought you just said preprinted materials get handed out at the conference . . . and what are these evaluation sheets? Are they the same thing as the reply cards?
Address on mailing envelopes: Sarah will let you know which.	Sarah who? When will she let me know? When do these things have to be in the mail, anyway?
Reply cards must fit into mailing envelopes.	Reply cards as in reply cards, or reply cards as in evaluation sheets? Give me a break.
Still to come: preconference material, a decision on return address, reply cards, and the conference agenda (we should have	What conference agenda?

Writer	Reader
about 200 of these at the conference registration table).	Oh, we should, should we? That's just great. I'll get right on it.
It's important that we take Ezra's concerns about price very seriously.	WHO IS EZRA?
As I mentioned, our phone conversation last week underscored how important his input is.	What phone conversation? Why are you telling me about price? Price of what? The conference? The materials?
This should wrap it up.	You can't be serious.
I'm sure you can handle everything from here on.	Piece of cake. Your wish is my command.
I'm leaving tomorrow for a three-week tour of our Asian subsidiaries, followed by some vacation time. See you at the conference.	Wait just a minute here. Who's in charge of this? Am I supposed to do all of this myself? I'm supposed to *be* at this conference? Who else was at this stupid meeting, anyway?

This is the fallout from bad writing: bad reading. Bad reading from a reader who seems to learn less and less as he goes, not more and more. A reader caught up in his own reactions rather than in the message. We can blame only the writer. The writer's monologue causes the reader's.

The manager uses the page to think out loud, thereby failing to communicate clearly. The employee spends time and energy deciphering rather than doing. The job isn't getting done—it's stuck in verbal limbo. The employee resents the task, and resents the manager for making it all so difficult.

You're probably thinking: Come on, now. Isn't this just a little bit exaggerated? Hartwig's replacement could get help. He could ask other people.

But he shouldn't have to. Business writing should do its job without requiring the services of outside interpreters. The reader should not need to fall back on someone who will explain what the document really means, what it should have said, what it *meant* to say.

In order to write you must make certain assumptions about your audience's involvement, receptivity, and willingness to take on the twin tasks of reading and doing. We rarely take the time we need to examine those assumptions from the reader's point of view.

Every document you write is part of a paper trail you leave for others to follow. Presumably you want them to do so. If not, it's impolitic to write in the first place; you hold a meeting instead, maybe behind closed doors. You purposely decide *not* to leave a trail. That is not the case here, however. Nor is it in most business writing. You write in order to leave a record.

You push your pencil across the page. The words add up and line up—but do the ideas? You are not managing the movement of verbal piecework along an assembly line. You are negotiating the movement of ideas, the interplay of two minds: yours and the reader's.

Your job is to turn this:

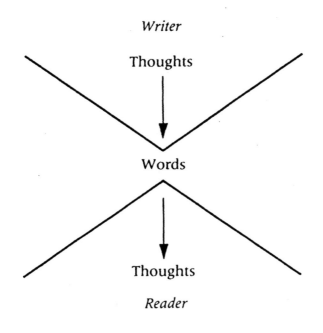

Writer

Thoughts

Words

Thoughts

Reader

into this:

Writer

Thoughts

Reader

Carla Mendez meant to be helpful. She wrote to instruct. To record. To clarify. But the ideas were not managed well; nor were the people. Had she delayed her Asian departure for a day she would have had Bob Hartwig or his replacement camped out on her doorstep, memo in hand, requesting additional information. Or she would have called another meeting to repeat the substance of the first one. More time wasted, both in the meeting and in writing the memo that inevitably would have followed to summarize it.

Imagine how much time corporate America wastes trying to decipher the meaning of the memos, letters, and reports stacked high on its collective desk. The job isn't getting done.

WRITER'S MIND, READER'S MIND —WHAT GOES ON?

Few writers think about what's going on in the reader's mind at the precise moment of reading. The diagrams above illustrate that reading consists of analyzing the words on the page to find the ideas behind them. As hard as it may be to accept, the reader is not riveted by your thoughts or dazzled by the elegance of your style. He's operating on a far more pedestrian plane. He's focused on the words, punctuation, paragraphs, headings, and any number of other "mechanical" considerations. He's using these to understand the context, establish logical links, and negotiate the sequence of sentences and ideas. Unless this process works smoothly, the reader gets distracted. He either gives up or rebels, and the writer's purpose, authority, and credibility are the casualties.

What about the writer? What's going on in that mind

at the precise moment of writing? A fishing expedition. Lots of casting about, probing beneath the surface of the topic in order to reel the thoughts in.

What Mendez Thought	*What She Wrote*
What do we need at the conference?	At the conference we need 100 blank manila envelopes, the preprinted material, a sample registration form, and reply cards.
Anything else?	We'll also need 75 manila envelopes containing preprinted materials, plus 100 evaluation sheets.
When do we need to mail preconference materials?	Preconference materials need to be mailed by May 30.
Which envelopes should we use?	Envelopes for this mailing should be the ones with the new design as approved.
What's included in preconference material packet?	Preconference material packet includes: preprinted materials, sample registration forms, and reply cards/evaluation sheets.
Whose name gets put on mailing envelopes?	Address on mailing envelopes: Sarah will let you know which.

What Mendez Thought	*What She Wrote*
How big should reply cards be?	Reply cards must fit into mailing envelopes.
What's left?	Still to come: preconference material, a decision on return address, reply cards, and the conference agenda (we should have about 200 of these at the conference registration table).
How do we deal with Ezra's concerns about price?	It's important that we take Ezra's concerns about price very seriously. As I mentioned, our phone conversation last week underscored how important his input is.
Anything else?	This should wrap it up. I'm sure you can handle everything from here on.
What about my trip?	I'm leaving tomorrow for a three-week tour of our Asian subsidiaries, followed by some vacation time. See you at the conference.

Seeing the writer's mind exposed like this makes you realize how far apart manager and employee are. At one point in the example above the reader anxiously asks,

"Sarah who? When will she let me know? When do these things have to be in the mail, anyway?" The manager's bizarre response: "Reply cards must fit into mailing envelopes." Dialogue indeed.

Imagine trying to get a joke you heard only half of:

A: [*Mutter*]
B: What seems to be the problem?
A: [*Mutter*]
B: What happens in these dreams?
A: [*Mutter*]
B: The problem is simple. You're too tense.*

When you look at this latter treatment of the memo, questions and answers together, it's as if you're attending the very meeting yourself. Had you been present the conversation might have gone very much like this one. Not a monologue or even a dialogue, but a press conference. A flurry of questions, some political ("How do we deal with Ezra's concerns about price?"), some piggybacking off of others ("Anything else?"), some practical ("Which envelopes should we use?"). Asked in no particular order and answered in kind.

It's now easy to spot this document as a by-product of what I call the "divine dictation" school of writing: you write down what comes to you in the order in which it comes to you. Maybe that's the order in which things

---

* A: Doctor, you've got to help me.
  B: What seems to be the problem?
  A: I have terrible nightmares every night.
  B: What happens in these dreams?
  A: Well, one night I dream I'm a tepee, and the next night I dream I'm a wigwam.
  B: The problem is simple. You're two tents.

happened; maybe it's simply the order in which you remember them (whatever order that is). Such a method provides useful data, but that's all—raw data. Grist for the writer's mill, certainly, but a far cry from the loaf of bread your reader was expecting.

In short, Carla Mendez's memo isn't a memo, and it isn't ready for reading.

How to fix it? The first thing to do is recognize—and learn to respect—not one but two conversations: the one you have with the reader and the one you have with yourself.

The second thing to do is learn to figure out which is which. That's what the management of thinking is all about.

CHAPTER THREE

The Management of Thinking

Ironically, when you write you put the reader-writer dialogue at risk. After all, you're not writing "to" anybody. On the contrary: you're writing to a legal pad, or the back of an envelope, or a computer screen. Your focus is a flat rectangular surface one or two feet in front of you. The data is right at hand. Your reader, by contrast, is across the hall or halfway around the world. You glimpse him only in your imagination—if you remember to look, that is.

No one in his right mind would describe writing as an efficient process. Inefficiency, however, is the least of it. The writing process deceives. It tends to foster in each writer the tenacious illusion that he is writing to the reader, when in reality he is writing mainly to himself.

It's often true that in the first stages of creativity the dynamic between writer and topic is more vivid than the dynamic between writer and reader. It's essential, however, to shift your focus from writer-topic to writer-reader, and to do so early in the writing process. I advocate shifting very early indeed: before you write the first draft. It's the best way to avoid mistaking your own analytical rantings for a reader-based dialogue.

The vast majority of writing problems that I have seen stem from precisely this sort of mistaken identity. The writer mistakes himself for the reader, and then proceeds to write to this motivated, knowledgeable, supportive audience of one. This audience bears little resemblance to the real reader, who, likely as not, is frazzled, inadequately informed, and inherently skeptical.

This chapter shows how to use writing as a bridge between thinking and communicating. What follows is a method to help you keep the monologue of thinking separate from the dialogue of writing. It involves taking an aerial view of the writing process—and a strategic approach to the entire managerial landscape in which you do your job.

THINKING THE RIGHT THINGS

In the previous chapter we saw the vast managerial chasm that separates the business writer and reader. I showed you a document that did more harm than good because it was written from the manager's perspective, not the employee's. The manager went from thoughts to words with nary a glance in the reader's direction.

Such myopia is understandable, given the intense concentration that writing demands. But writing requires more than concentration; it requires focus.

I define concentration as the ability to think hard, and focus as the ability to think about the right things. As a writer and manager you need both.

But what are the "right things"? Won't they vary from document to document and from writer to writer? They may, but surprisingly little. Every writer, for example, thinks about what he's writing; he thinks about his message. He thinks about why he's writing; he thinks about the purpose of his document. He also thinks about his reader, his audience; but as I've said, this is harder than it sounds.

For many business writers the list ends there, and it shouldn't. There are three additional "right things," and in my view they constitute the bridge between thinking and communicating, between writer and reader. They help you shift from data to dialogue. I call these Situation, Introduction, and Question.

The six "right things," then, are Message, Audience, Purpose, Situation, Introduction, and Question. These do not exactly trip lightly off the tongue, so for easy reference I refer to them by the acronym MAPSIQ. I've experimented with the alternatives for years . . . SPAMIQ? SPAMQI? APSIQM? SIQMAP? The order of the elements matters not at all.

What does matter, however, is that you think systematically about each element *before* you begin to write. If you do, you'll be considering the reader's perspective as well as your own—and you'll be able to tell which is which. As a result, you can structure your writing as a reader-based dialogue rather than a writer-based monologue.*

Every document, after all, is a response to an issue

---

* I've borrowed the terms "reader-based" and "writer-based" from rhetorician Linda Flower.

raised before, whether on paper or in a meeting or in the elevator. Every document is a response to a problem or opportunity requiring that some consensus be achieved or action taken. No one comes to work in the morning and suddenly decides that it would be fun to write a budget, say, or document the inventory-flow problem. Your document is itself part of a dialogue.

MAPSIQ: Message, Audience, Purpose, Situation, Introduction, and Question. The most critical of these is Audience, since the reader's perspective is ultimately what you are striving to address. MAPSIQ forces you to reckon with your reader before you write your first sentence; doing so may save you several drafts.

Here's a look at each component of MAPSIQ. (On page 45 we'll apply them to an actual document so that you can see how they work.) Incidentally, MAPSIQ turns out to be a useful antidote for writer's block. No matter how stumped you are by the topic or the task of writing, chances are that with MAPSIQ you can always find somewhere to start and something to say. There's no reason for you to start with Message, or end with Question. Start where it makes sense, or where it's easiest—talk to yourself or talk to the reader. If you're not getting anywhere, start somewhere else.

MAPSIQ

MESSAGE The Punchline	What is the major point? What, in one sentence, is the content of what you have to say? If the audience remembers only one thing, what must it be?
AUDIENCE Motivational Profile	Who? How many? How different? What do they want? What is their relationship to you, and what is yours to them? What do you want it to be? How can you use this document to achieve that relationship?
PURPOSE Your Objective	What is the purpose of the document? What *must* you accomplish? If you're successful, what will happen? If you're not, what will happen? What do you want the audience to *do*, or be ready to do, after reading your document?
SITUATION Yours	Why are *you* writing this document, and not someone else? What are the pressures on you —professional, political, and personal—that make this difficult? What else is on your mind that distracts you from this task?
INTRODUCTION Audience's	If you were making an oral presentation about this topic, how would you introduce it? What, in a nutshell, is the problem or issue you're writing about? What background information can you provide in two or three sentences that will lead directly to the question you're addressing?
QUESTION	What's the *central* question that your document addresses?

M = Message. This is the punchline, the answer. To get it you need to ask yourself some hard questions:

What is my major point? What, in one sentence, is the content of what I have to say? If the reader remembers only one thing, what must it be?

Sounds easy, but it isn't. Typically you're so close to your subject that it's hard to focus on the "take-away." Or else you're so enamored of the document that you can't imagine the reader taking away only one message. Be humble—and realistic—and consider yourself lucky if your reader takes away the one message you most wanted and needed him to. Consider yourself more than lucky; consider yourself skillful.

A = Audience. This component is trickier, more wily. Here you need to sketch what amounts to a motivational profile of your reader, in order to figure out as precisely as possible how he'll read your document— and how he'll react. A participant in one of my writing seminars, a lawyer whom I tried to cross-examine on the question of audience, crowed gleefully, "Who cares about the audience?" Clearly he did not, and his writing amounted to little more than an airtight seal to keep the reader out. (This gentleman is now assembling widgets in South Dakota.)

In figuring out your audience you need to identify what you know—and don't know. Doing so will mean answering questions like these:

Who? How many? How different? What do they want? What is my relationship to them, and what is theirs to me? What do I *want* our relationship to be? How can I use this document to achieve that relationship? How does my message differ from the message they're expecting?

P = Purpose. This is your objective in writing. Or rather, your objectives: there is always more than one, and the more of them you identify, the better you fortify yourself for the actual writing task. It's a good idea to identify not only the most concrete and immediate goals, but also the more abstract and far-reaching ones. You'll need to answer these questions:

What is the purpose of this document? What *must* I accomplish? What will happen if I'm successful? What will happen if I'm not? What do I want the audience to *do*, or be ready to do, after reading the document?

It's important to note the difference between purpose and message. Think of the purpose as the hidden or not-so-hidden agenda *behind* the message.

A: I fell into a vat full of chocolate.
B: That's terrible. . . . What did you do?
A: I yelled "Fire!"
B: You yelled "Fire"? Why did you do that?
A: Because no one would have saved me if I'd yelled "Chocolate!"

Assessing your purpose, in other words, helps you figure out the best way to phrase your message. It helps you decide how forceful you should be.

Looking at Audience and Purpose together helps you think about one of the most elusive characteristics of writing: tone. For most people, tone is what the writing ends up sounding like when they've finished writing. It just happens. I offer this definition: Tone is how you want to be remembered. Tone is the whiff of you, a sort of verbal cologne. It lingers in the air after the reader finishes reading, and it often stays with the reader longer than the actual message does. For this reason it's worth forethought.

S = Situation. Here you have a chance to do something few writers take the time to do: analyze the particular challenges that a given writing task poses. When you do, you identify the places where you're most likely to be talking to yourself rather than the reader.

> Why am *I* writing this document, and not someone else? What are the pressures on *me*—professional, political, and personal—that make this difficult? What else is on my mind that distracts me from this task?

The pressures besetting you can run the gamut. Some are directly related to the document (an unrealistic deadline), while others are tangential (the work you had to put on hold in order to write this document; the people you must contact but can't locate; the risk of overstating or understating your message). Some have nothing to do with the writing task you face (a sick child perhaps, or other family concerns). Whether professional or personal, these pressures should be isolated from the task of writing.

Acknowledging them—even jotting them down—

has two important benefits. First, you externalize these pressures. You get them out of your head and onto a piece of paper so that they don't swim endlessly in the brain, a constant distraction. Second, you give the pressures a name—and in so doing you may be able to formulate a strategy for dealing with them. Writing them down helps you figure them out. The very act of writing thus becomes an act of problem-solving.

I = Introduction.   Here is where the writer-reader dialogue begins. It's the place to visualize the reader actually hearing your words—the words you would use if speaking face to face. Your goal is a brief, logical launching of the topic. You set the stage, you provide a context.

If I were making an oral presentation about this topic, how would I introduce it? What, in a nutshell, is the problem or issue I'm writing about? What background information can I provide in two or three sentences that will lead directly to the question I'm addressing?

Writers in the heat of creation abhor the notion of the nutshell. They're experts on the topic, and they assume that the reader wants to be an expert too. My experience, however, tells me they are confusing their need to tell with the reader's need to know. The trick is learning how much the reader needs. And one way to find out is to step back and give the bare bones, the scaffolding. Doing so may save a lot of time later.

The introduction should lead, logically and inescapably, to the question. The reason is that you've used it to set the stage for the question.

Q = Question. This is the question your reader would ask after hearing the introduction. The question on his mind—and on yours. The question to which your document is the answer.

To figure it out, look back at the introduction and the message. What question can you formulate that will connect the two? The introduction should prompt the question; the question should prompt the message.*

You know you're thinking logically when Introduction, Question, and Message are tightly linked, with a kind of lockstep logic.

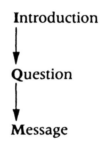

Introduction

Question

Message

PUTTING MAPSIQ TO WORK

MAPSIQ directs your thinking about the document, turning a writer-based monologue into a reader-based dialogue.

Now that we've discussed MAPSIQ in the abstract, let's put it to work. The conference memo from the last chapter does nicely.

I usually start with Audience.

---

*Barbara Minto's *Pyramid Principle* (London: Minto International Inc., 1981) has been useful in helping me refine my own ideas about how to structure a well-crafted introduction.

Audience

Bob Hartwig. New—been here about three weeks. Likes working for me but is impatient with the more mundane aspects of the job. Bright, aggressive, but not excited by detail, and definitely not excited about handling the conference, since so much attention to detail is required. Therefore, I must spell out instructions but must make them sound very organized and doable, since I won't be available for consultation.

Net: Analyzing the Audience forces Mendez to step back and think of the conference from Hartwig's perspective as well as from hers.

Purpose

To finalize instructions on preparation of conference materials so that people can get this done in my absence. If successful, Hartwig et al. will get all this stuff done correctly and on time without bothering me with details I don't have time for. If this memo fails, Hartwig screws up (and so do I); conference materials jeopardized; cost overruns; more work later—frantic last-minute scramble, sloppy work inevitable. And who will be in charge of all the pieces? Not me.

Net: Assessing the Purpose provides Mendez with a strategy: this memo must be the baton in a relay race—not a boomerang that comes back at her after she sends it forth. She has to write it in such a way that she becomes dispensable. Tone, therefore, should be breezy and conversational. She must persuade Hartwig how little he needs her.

Situation

I'm leaving tomorrow for three weeks and I need to tie up all the loose ends on these conference materials. Can't spend much time on this now, and can't leave any questions unaddressed. This thing landed in my lap last month and I haven't even had a chance to think about it until this week. . . . Why they didn't turn this over to Conference Planning I'll never know. Hartwig can handle it, but he won't be very happy. Too bad. I have too much else to do. Haven't even begun the proposal I said I'd have by this afternoon. And I need to get out of here by 6:00 at the latest—need to get to the dry cleaner's before it closes, and the shoe repair. Haircut will have to wait . . . I wonder what a haircut would be like in Hong Kong.

Net: Life is too short; I've got other fish to fry. Notice how the thinking here gets closer and closer to Carla, and further and further from the problem at hand? It turns out that there are two problems at hand: Carla's pressured preparations for the trip and her pressured preparations for the conference. They have nothing to do with each other, but they are inextricably linked in Carla's mind and will remain so—under a bright neon light that says "Pressure"—until she forces herself to tackle them one at a time.

Introduction

We have a conference coming up in July. As you know, we met on May 2 to discuss preparation of conference materials. I'll be out of the country between now and

July, and so you're going to do the lion's share of this preparation. So you need to know in detail what to focus on to get all the materials completed.

Net: The writer thinks about things as if she were the reader. The writer anticipates the reader's need for a context; the writer respects the reader's need for dialogue.

Question

What do we need to focus on to get the materials completed?

Net: See how easily, how logically the question flows from the introduction? So easily, in fact, that it probably won't appear anywhere in the document itself. It won't need to. Indeed, if the introduction is tightly reasoned, the question is often left unsaid by the writer. But said or unsaid, it must be *felt* as surely as it would be if the reader were present, asking it. And it must point directly to the message.

Message

Focus on the budget, the last-minute design issues, the preconference mailing, and the conference materials themselves.

Net: The memo will contain instructions about what to do, structured for the reader's benefit rather than for the writer's convenience.

Look again at Introduction, Question, and Message.

Introduction:	We have a conference coming up in July. As you know, we met on May 2 to discuss preparation of conference materials. I'll be out of the country between now and July, and so you're going to do the lion's share of this preparation. So you need to know in detail what to focus on to get all the materials completed.
Question:	What do we need to focus on to get the materials completed?
Message:	Focus on the budget, the last-minute design issues, the preconference mailing, and the conference materials themselves.

Behold. A conversation, a dialogue with the reader. It is stimulated by the introduction, focused by the question, and addressed by the message. If we think about the relationship of Introduction, Question, and Message, a whole new way of writing emerges: a way of writing based on the interactive relationship between writer and reader. And with it comes a whole new memo, structured to reveal this relationship.

Revision

Date:	May 6
To:	Bob Hartwig
From:	Carla Mendez
Subject:	July 2 Conference

Introduction → In our May 2 meeting we discussed preparation of July 2 conference materials. I'll be
out of the office until then, so here's a recap
of what you need to focus on to get the job
done:

Message →
- the budget
- the last-minute design issues
- the preconference mailing
- the conference materials themselves
(for both registration table and opening forum)

Budget

Ezra felt strongly that we need to come out at least 10%
under budget on the preparation of all the materials discussed below. He has done this kind of conference planning before and understands the numbers, so by all means
make use of him.

Design Issues

- reply cards must fit mailing envelopes
- return address on envelopes—Sarah will let you
know which. Contact her in a week if she hasn't contacted you.
- agenda—still being designed. Ezra is in charge and
will get this to you ASAP. Contact him if you have
questions.

Preconference Mailing

These documents, inserted in the new envelopes (the ones with new design recently approved by headquarters), must be in the mail no later than May 30:

- 100 sets of preprinted materials
- 100 registration forms
- 100 reply cards
- 100 evaluation sheets

Conference Materials

At the registration table we'll need:

- 100 blank empty manila envelopes
- 100 sets of preprinted materials
- 1 sample registration form, for reference only
- 100 reply cards
- 200 copies of conference agenda

At the opening forum we'll need:

- 75 blank manila envelopes, each containing a set of preprinted materials
- 100 evaluation sheets

This should wrap it up. I will not be easy to reach, so if you have any questions about what needs to get done, ask me before 5:30 this evening. In an emergency, my secretary will be able to phone or fax a message to me, but keep in mind that there will be thirteen time zones between us.

Thanks for your help. See you at the conference.

Is this memo now perfect, you ask? No. (It will be closer to perfection after we've dealt with it again in chapter 5.) But it has come a long way—from laundry list to work plan.

Along with the increase in verbal clarity comes an increase in managerial authority. The manager conveys more than the instructions; she conveys a sense of her self—a self who's organized and clear, and who expects her staff to be organized and clear too. The manager motivates by communicating her power. She has used words and ideas as a way to manage people. She has done so by balancing the twin demands of data and dialogue.

The original memo signaled nothing so much as a vague (though well-intentioned) supervisory fog.

MAPSIQ helps separate the two conflicting voices of monologue and dialogue in you.

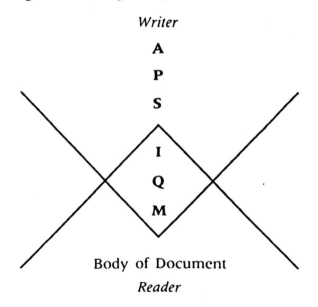

Writer

A

P

S

I

Q

M

Body of Document

Reader

Audience, Purpose, and Situation create the monologue. Introduction, Question, and Message create the dialogue, thereby helping sustain the managerial relationship.

Assessing Audience, Purpose, and Situation will help you plan Introduction, Question, and Message. This isn't to say that you won't hop back and forth from element to element; you probably will. But at least you'll know how to identify where you are, where you're going, and how to get there.

Most people spend their writing lives spinning their wheels. MAPSIQ helps you focus. It gives you traction.

CHAPTER FOUR

Negotiating with the Reader

Consider this advice, attached to the bulletin boards if not the psyches of business writers across the land:

K.I.S.S. (Keep it Simple, Stupid.)

What a curious perspective that tidy little maxim reveals. You can interpret it in two ways: (1) as a form of self-rebuke, a sheepish admission that you're usually too confused to write clearly; or (2) as a cynical reminder that you must write "down" to your lowly reader. Either way it patronizes.

What does "simple" mean? Easy for the reader. But what does that mean? Easy to get off the page. But what does *that* mean? How do you write so that writing is easy to get off the page?

Too often writers think that simple means simplistic, watered down, less than full strength. I offer a different definition. "Simple" writing is concentrated, distilled, synthesized for the reader. Not watered down, but rather, boiled down and refined until the usable essence remains. This comment, attributed by some to nineteenth-century writer Madame de Staël, captures it best: "Pardon, my dear daughter, for such a long letter. I did not have time to write a short one."

In business, effective writing requires mastery of the short one. The reader won't read a long document, it's true, but there are other reasons. A short one—concentrated, distilled, synthesized for the reader—also helps the writer. The skill involved in writing a short one is the same skill that managers need to solve business problems.

ELOQUENT BOUNDARIES, USEFUL CONSTRAINTS

In the management consulting world, distillation is a way of life. Consultants solve problems and then present their solutions. They do this by an ingenious method borrowed, no doubt, from the hard sciences and from philosophy: problems are treated as questions that need answers.

This may sound simple and straightforward; I assure you that it is not. *Problems fester; questions focus. Problems nag; questions probe. Problems complicate; questions clarify.*

Problems Fester, Questions Focus

Problems	*Questions*
Increasing competition	**What**'s the competition doing? **Why** has it been so successful? **How** can we retaliate?

Problems	*Questions*
Low productivity	**What** are our productivity figures this quarter? **Why** is productivity lower? **How** can we increase it?
Underperforming assets	**What's** in the portfolio? **Why** are the assets performing so poorly? **How** can we offset the effects of underperforming assets?

The transformation of problems into questions is a powerful problem-solving tool in its own right. The thinking process becomes a disciplined inquiry shaped by eloquent boundaries. These boundaries constrain us, to be sure; but they are "useful constraints" (a wonderful phrase of poet Ruth Danon). They define the size and shape of the problem, and in so doing they define the size and shape of the solution.

Questions anticipate the answers; they lay out a path for the problem-solver to follow. But they do more. They also anticipate the *audience*; they lay out a path for the *reader* to follow. They literally "speak" and thus trigger a response. Questions trigger dialogue. Problems are solitary and internal, but questions are social. They summon the answers, and they summon the reader as well. They bring us back out into the world—the world of action, of doing—which is precisely where business writers need to be.

Why? Because the business world is about problems and solutions and actions. It's about fixing things that are broken and improving things that aren't as good as they could be. It's about figuring out *how* to fix things, *how* to make them better. It's about commerce and making money, of course, but it concerns itself with the "how" of life as well.

Identifying the right question is key to the entire problem-solving process, because it connects you to the answer. Identifying the right question is also key to the writing process, because it connects you to the reader and the message.

I once worked with an apoplectic engineer, a Ph.D. from MIT, who had five hundred pages of information from which to write a report on the economics of nuclear technology by ten A.M. *the next day.* This writer had a topic—the economics of nuclear technology. He also had two problems: a punishing deadline and a senior management audience whom he did not know. "There's too much data!" he screamed at me. "How can I organize it by tomorrow?"

That was the Situation. That was all he would talk about. In other words, he was stuck in a data-driven monologue. I tried to get him to focus instead on the dialogue. I said, "In my experience, too much data usually means not enough synthesis. What does the reader want to know?"

"Management wants to know how to fund the next two reactors we're going to build."

Now, at least, we had a Question to work with. "What's the answer?" I asked him. "How *should* management fund the next two reactors?" He rifled through the five-inch stack of papers on his desk. "It's here somewhere. . . . I found it." He pulled a page triumphantly from the bottom. There, clear as day, was the Message: three neat columns showing the proposed sources of funding for the reactors.

"This is your report," I said, holding up the sheet he'd pulled. Then I pointed to the pile on his desk and said, "And that's the appendix."

The report went out at nine the next morning. It was fourteen pages long. The title had changed from "The Economics of Nuclear Technology" to "A and B Reactor Project: How to Fund?" The first page was an introduction that set the stage for the question "How to fund?" The second page was a verbal summary of the answer. Page three was the three-column numerical answer. Page four described the appendix materials which followed. These had been boiled down from five hundred pages to ten.

The writer sent me a copy and asked for feedback. I called to congratulate him on the fine job he'd done, and made one suggestion: Next time, add a cover memo inviting the reader to contact you if there are questions or comments. There may be—especially since you distilled such a dense and forbidding mound of data into such a well-crafted, accessible dialogue. Exploit the dialogue; one of your Purposes in writing, surely, is to sustain a highly visible relationship with senior management.

Identifying the right question is central to the entire writing process, yet it is no easy thing. It involves creating and sustaining a dialogue with the reader—on the right subject, at the right level of abstraction, with the right amount of supporting detail.

CHOOSING THE QUESTION

To choose the question is to "choose" the answer as well—or at least its size and shape. The question drives the answer, and it also provides the eloquent boundaries for the document itself. The question drives the document, and only three questions matter. MAPSIQ helps you figure out which one matters most.

The Question Drives the Document

Question	Answer	Document
WHAT	Here's what is	**Description** Emphasis on documenting, providing a record, giving background
WHY?	Here's what we think, believe	**Diagnosis** Emphasis on evaluating, judging, making a case
HOW?	Here's what we recommend; here's what has to be done	**Prescription** Emphasis on listing actions, giving orders

The question drives the document, and MAPSIQ drives the question.

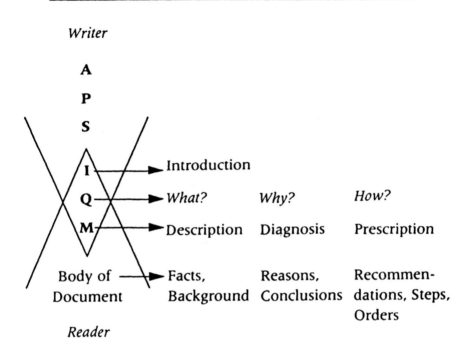

The question you choose dictates the structure and flow of your document. If you pose a What question, then your document should present the pertinent facts. If you pose a Why question, then your document should present a conclusion or judgment supported by those facts. If you pose a How question, then your document should present a recommendation or plan of action supported by your conclusion which, in turn, is supported by the facts.

WHAT?	WHY?	HOW?
		Prescription
	Diagnosis	Diagnosis
Description	Description	Description

By this logic, a description is the most basic and, in a way, the most rudimentary form of information. A diagnosis represents the information distilled at a higher level, and a recommendation represents the information distilled at a higher level still.

LOOK THROUGH THE WORDS

The question takes on monumental importance; it is the mechanism by which you examine your topic, the vise with which you hold it in order to build the document. The tighter the grip, the more concentrated the question, the answer, and the document become.

MAPSIQ, then, is a tool to help you decide which question works best and which answer, or Message, is most appropriate. Given the variables of Audience, Purpose, and Situation, your document will require a What, Why, or How question. The answer will be either a description of facts, a judgment based on the facts, or a recommendation based on the conclusion and on the facts.

A cautionary note: Don't be deceived by variations in word choice. Look through the words. "What can we do to improve distribution?" may sound like a descriptive question, but it's actually a prescriptive How question. The answer will be a recommendation, a plan for action: "Centralize the distribution into a hub-and-spoke structure."

Here's another example: "What happened at the last project meeting?" This question could prompt two kinds of answers, two kinds of documents: descriptive or diagnostic.

If descriptive, the document would be a chronological, blow-by-blow account of who said what—the minutes of the meeting:

> The meeting took place at 4:00 p.m. on Thursday, January 4. All the systems engineers were present, as well as the inventory manager and the distribution manager. The project manager led the discussion. He began by asking each of us to give a brief overview of the subroutine, followed by a comment on how the new software package was working. Alan spoke first. He distributed handouts showing how the new package differed from the old, and highlighting problem areas. One of these was the coding procedure. . . .

If diagnostic, the document would be the writer's conclusions about the meeting:

> The meeting covered many topics, but the only pertinent discussion for us was the final one, about the inventory backlog. Most of the distribution managers seemed to favor a change to Just-in-Time processes. There was no vote, but the majority of comments supported this approach. . . .

Which is appropriate, description or diagnosis? Only by surveying Audience, Purpose, and Situation will you be able to decide. Your knowledge of the reader in particular will be useful. The descriptive version—the minutes themselves—is entirely appropriate for the members present, but not for the head of your division. The diagnostic version—your judgment of the value of the meeting—would appeal to a senior audience far more than to those who were present at the meeting.

The important thing to remember is that What, Why, and How are species of questions; it is not the exact words that matter, but rather, the logical framework they point toward.

I suggest that in planning your document you try your questions several different ways, using different wordings, until you find what works best. You'll be forcing yourself to see the topic and the message from several different logical perspectives. You are in effect forcing yourself to engage in a dialogue with the reader about the topic. There is no better way to clarify what you mean to say, and to think through the implications of saying it. There is no better way to rehearse the process of getting the ideas off the page, into people's minds, and onto their agendas. Manage the question well and you've begun to implement the answer.

Here's a diagnostic memo—it addresses the question Why. This writer has distilled his remarks into a useful synthesis.

Date:

To:

From:

Subject: Compensation Plan—Results of
Competitive Analysis

As you know, we conducted this study to understand why prospective employees give our compensation package comparatively low marks.

After reviewing the analysis (attached), I've con-
cluded that our package is inferior to our competitors'
plans in three areas:

- Our bonus scale is consistently lower than theirs.
- Our health care benefits exclude eye care and
  dental care; theirs include them.
- Our tuition reimbursement policy is far more re-
  strictive than theirs.

I'll call you tomorrow to get your reactions and plan
the next steps.

Attachment

In this memo, the introduction ("As you know, we
conducted this study to understand why prospective
employees give our compensation package comparatively low marks") actually *contains* the question. The
question appears nowhere on the page, and yet it is
clearly the organizing principle of the entire memo. The
document presents the writer's assessment of the package's shortcomings.

That assessment is supported by the actual findings of

the study itself. This is the raw data of the document, the descriptive ingredients put through a diagnostic sieve. The reader who wishes to examine them individually may; but no one has to do so to understand this memo—or to act on it.

This manager is in charge of the study, the results—and the next steps.

The question drives the document. It also determines the impact you have as both a writer and a manager. Here's a document, written by your new vice-president of marketing, that isn't so successful.

Date:
To:
From:
Subject: San Francisco Meeting

The regional marketing managers are all attending the first annual meeting on March 12. The main speaker will be George Thomas, former director of the National Marketing Trade Group. Some of the managers have asked Mr. Thomas to meet with them after his speech in order to discuss their marketing strategies. Those meetings are scheduled to start right after his speech.

They have also asked the head of a marketing consulting firm, A. A. Reynolds, to meet with them in order to explore possibilities for coordinating all the efforts throughout the region, and to see if there can be a greater tie-in with other regions.

As you may or may not know, I recently hired a new marketing publications manager, Alice Kearny.

She has spent the past three months traveling to all the regional offices, working closely with all the marketing managers. It turns out that Alice used to work for Reynolds. In addition, she knows George Thomas. As far as I know, she is the only person in the company who has these contacts.

As a result, it might make sense to ask Alice to attend the March 12 meeting.

Your first reaction is probably irritation: "So what?" Your second is probably increased irritation: "Are you writing this to ask me if Alice Kearny can go, or to tell me that you've already decided? If you've already decided, why are you writing this? Are you trying to illustrate what a dazzling staff you've put together—or show me how spotty our contacts were until you and Kearny came along?"

It's not until the last sentence of the third paragraph that you sense where the writer is going ("she is the only person in the company who has these contacts"). Not until the last sentence of the whole document ("it might make sense to ask Alice to attend the March 12 meeting") do you know what's on his mind. Presumably, it's something like:

Let's make sure that Alice Kearny attends the March 12 marketing meeting.

If that is in fact the message (we're assuming it is; but what on earth is it doing at the very end?), the purpose of the memo is to get you to endorse, if not authorize,

Kearny's attendance. If that is in fact the purpose, then the document is prescriptive; it makes a recommendation. If it makes a recommendation, then the question is How.

Now, on to the specific wording of the question. Given all that we've said so far, what question would prompt this answer: "Let's make sure that Alice Kearny attends the March 12 marketing meeting"? Surely, something like:

How can we ensure that we get the most out of the marketing meeting?

And so the question and the message would be:

Question: How can we ensure that we get the most out of the marketing meeting?

Message: Let's make sure that Alice Kearny attends.

So far so good. The body of the memo, presumably, will tell us the reason or reasons. Why *should* we make sure that Kearny attends? Because she's the only one who knows the speakers—but is that all? Let's come back to the body after we've tackled the introduction.

The question implies, subtly, a lack or deficiency: without something added, we may not get the most out of the meeting. (I've read between the lines in order to write the introduction. This may sound like cheating, but it isn't: writing an introduction often means doing precisely that—reading between the lines, examining what's implicit to see if you need to make it explicit. Often you do.)

Introduction: The first annual national marketing
meeting brings together our regional
managers with two of the country's
top marketing experts, George Thomas
and A. A. Reynolds. The meeting has
two objectives: to develop regional
strategies and to explore ways to coordinate them more effectively. See
the attached agenda.

A meeting of this magnitude is an
important new effort for us. I'd like to
ensure that we get the most out of the
speakers and the managers.

See what happened? The search for an introduction
meant distilling the gist of the entire document. It
meant acknowledging a broader purpose than simply
getting you to authorize Kearny's attendance. That
broader purpose was to get you to appreciate how
important the meeting is, how well it could go if all the
pieces are in place, and how effective Kearny's presence could be.

This introduction leads directly to the question.

Introduction: . . . I'd like to ensure that we get the
most out of the speakers and the man-
agers.

Question: How can we ensure that we get the
most out of the speakers and the managers?

Now that we have a workable introduction—one that forcefully takes both the writer and the reader into account—we can look back at the body of the memo, which contains the reason for authorizing Kearny to attend. Again, the implicit is made explicit.

Question: How can we ensure that we get the most out of the the marketing meeting?

Message: I recommend that we ask the new marketing publications manager, Alice Kearny, to attend.

Reader: Why?

Her presence will help the meeting start strong and stay cohesive.

Reader: Why? In what way?

She's a known quantity to both Thomas and Reynolds (she used to work for Reynolds and has known Thomas for years). In addition, she's highly regarded by all the regional managers.

Rewritten, this memo is an extended writer-reader dialogue triggered by the introduction. Every statement prompts a response addressed by the statement that follows.

Compare the old with the new. The original is what we charitably call a data dump: a vast heap of information in search of a purpose and structure.

Original

Date:
To:
From:
Subject: San Francisco Meeting

The regional marketing managers are all attending the first annual meeting on March 12. The main speaker will be George Thomas, former director of the National Marketing Trade Group. Some of the managers have asked Mr. Thomas to meet with them after his speech in order to discuss their marketing strategies. Those meetings are scheduled to start right after his speech.

They have also asked the head of a marketing consulting firm, A. A. Reynolds, to meet with them in order to explore possibilities for coordinating all the efforts throughout the region, and to see if there can be a greater tie-in with other regions.

As you may or may not know, I recently hired a new marketing publications manager, Alice Kearny. She has spent the past three months traveling to all the regional offices, working closely with all the marketing managers. It turns out that Alice used to work for Reynolds. In addition, she knows George Thomas. As far as I know, she is the only person in the company who has these contacts.

As a result, it might make sense to ask Alice to attend the March 12 meeting.

The document is descriptive from start to finish—subject line ("San Francisco Meeting") and punch line ("As a result, it might make sense to ask Alice to attend the March 12 meeting") and every line in between. The manager chronicles the facts. He doesn't interpret them, and he certainly doesn't take responsibility for them.

The manager follows the data. It leads him by the hand. See how halting his steps, how tentative his progress.

The revision, by contrast, is prescriptive. The document has been turned inside out and upside down. The end has become the beginning, and the information has been structured to foster a give-and-take between writer and reader.

Revision

Date:
To:
From:
Subject: National Marketing Meeting—
              Ensuring Success

The first annual national marketing meeting brings together our regional managers with two of the country's top marketing experts, George Thomas and A. A. Reynolds. The meeting has two objectives: to develop regional strategies and to explore ways to coordinate them more effectively. See the attached agenda.

A meeting of this magnitude is an important new effort for us. I'd like to take steps to ensure that we get the most out of the speakers and the managers.

I recommend that we ask the new marketing publications manager, Alice Kearny, to attend. Her presence will help the meeting start strong and stay cohesive:

- She's a known quantity to both Thomas and Reynolds: she used to work for Reynolds, and she has known Thomas for years.
- She's highly regarded by all the regional managers.

If you have further thoughts, please give me a call. Otherwise I'll assume you agree. I'm scheduled to meet with Alice next week and will speak with her about the meeting then.

Gone is the descriptive agenda that made up the first two paragraphs in the original. It's now an attachment. The new introduction is focused on the objectives of the meeting and how to attain them.

The manager recommends. He anticipates his recommendation in the subject line ("National Marketing Meeting—Ensuring Success"). He takes a risk. He presents a plan of action (invite Alice Kearny) supported by a belief ("Her presence will help the meeting start strong and stay cohesive"), which in turn is supported by facts (she knows both speakers, and the regional managers respect her).

The manager goes out on a limb, certainly—but look

how many layers of logic support him. See how confidently he moves, secure in the knowledge that he has reasoned his way carefully. He convinces because he is convincing.

The document ends forcefully. There's an invitation to continue the dialogue ("If you have further thoughts, please give me a call"); but he knows what he wants to do and why, and he's ready to do it.

Which manager would you rather have reporting to you?

THE QUESTION OF LEVERAGE

The two great sins of managerial writing are thinking on paper and being afraid to say what needs to be said. We've seen examples of both in this book, and the juxtaposition is ironic here as in life. In committing the first, you blaze a trail in the forest. In succumbing to the second, you camouflage it.

When you write, you discover your ideas and how invested you are in them. You also negotiate the risks of that investment. Do I really want to say that? Do I really want to say that *here*? Do I *really* want to say it this strongly? I can't say *that*. I can't say that in *this* document.

The risks are real—but they often make us weaken our writing in ways that backfire. The fear of political fallout can paralyze thought, writing, and the ability to manage effectively.

MAPSIQ dispassionately offers two perspectives. The

micro perspective allows you to think clearly about your message, and the macro perspective allows you to think clearly about its ramifications. Moreover, MAPSIQ allows you to think about these two things in parallel rather than as one seething mass. MAPSIQ keeps anxiety from preempting logical thought.

Writing is risky. Your ideas can be ignored, misunderstood, or sabotaged. I'd like to suggest, however, that the risks inherent in writing be viewed not in negative but in positive terms, as bases for choosing the degree of influence you wish to exert.

This, then, is the fourth question—the question that every business writer should have attached to his bulletin board and his psyche:

How directly do I want or need this document to influence action?

The way you answer that question will tell you a great deal about how much leverage to exert. It becomes another eloquent boundary, another useful constraint to add to the three—What, Why, How—you already have.

If, after thinking through MAPSIQ, you decide you wish to exert the greatest possible leverage, you will want to write a diagnostic or prescriptive document rather than a descriptive one. But if you decide that only minimal leverage is required or desirable, you will want to write a descriptive or diagnostic one. There may be times when it's best to focus on the Why even when you know the How; perhaps it makes sense politically to get the reader to the How in stages. These are the concerns every writer and manager must grapple with. It's best to know what you're grappling with, and why it matters.

In corporate life, writing is negotiating the movement of ideas through an organization. In order to do so successfully, you need to decide how much leverage to exert. The risks are real, but they should always be weighed against a fully developed thought process; they should never be allowed to short-circuit it. In other words, it pays to know what you want to say before you decide whether to say it.

CHAPTER FIVE

Using Space, Using Silence

Writing is a powerful bridge between thinking and communicating, as we've seen. MAPSIQ gives you an aerial view of the writing process and the political landscape in which you operate. It forces you to balance the demands of your data with the demands of the dialogue. It also helps you decide how to shape that dialogue for a given reader. But what good is the dialogue if you can't get the reader to hear it and take part in it?

We do not tend to think of print as a participatory medium. On the contrary. Print intimidates. The eyes glaze over, the mind wanders. The reader is somewhere else—perhaps he's thinking about the presentation he just gave, or the phone call he just finished, or the task force he's about to chair. How can he turn his attention from the stridency of the human voice to the silence of the printed page?

The reader has every right to feel daunted; consider the tasks before him. Your voice has been squashed flat, reduced to a series of marks on paper. Eyeing those marks, he must imagine their sounds. Scanning the page, he searches for meaning and purpose; he searches for the dialogue. He must work hard to construct it, to conceive it, in order for it to take place at all. He won't be willing to do it unless you help.

The development of writing transformed speech utterly and forever: it turned sound into sight. What had heretofore been spoken and heard could now be seen as well. The oral was made visible. This transformation of sounds into marks on a page, of vocal range into visual field, has staggering implications for writers and readers alike. Symbols stand in for sounds; the eye stands in for the ear. To put it another way, the eye becomes the gateway to the ear.

We have spent hundreds of years struggling with ways to best "capture" speech and dialogue on the printed page. This chapter discusses three methods—the essential three for business writers, in my view: space, headings, and bullet points. Use these well and you will do as much as any writer can to make the dialogue real to the reader. Why? You'll be in charge of the direction and pacing of the dialogue.

ATTEND TO SPEECH

When I begin to work with a client, even a client who wants help on writing, I attend to speech first. I listen hard. I assess how articulate the person is. By this I do not mean how large the speaker's vocabulary is. Vocabulary is only a part of it. I'm interested in something much broader. I want to know how comfortably, how easily, the speaker dips into the vast arsenal of communication devices at his disposal: words, gestures, intonation, a steady gaze, to name a few.

I listen hardest for silence. It tells me whether the

speaker knows I'm there. It situates us in a dialogue.

Conversation, an activity of extraordinary complexity, is made up of two essential ingredients: speech and the space around it, which is silence. The silence is there for a reason. It gives the speaker time to think, and it gives the listener time to react to what has just been said, and perhaps to respond. Silence gives weight to utterance. We tend to be afraid of it; it makes us uncomfortable. This is unfortunate, because our fear too often results in a conversational style that is rude and dysfunctional in the extreme: the speaker engages in a breathless, self-centered monologue at breakneck speed. There's not a pause in sight; he doesn't need one; he's on a roll. He might as well be talking to a brick wall.

Writing is an extension of speech. A written document is made up of two essential ingredients: words and the space around them. The space is there for a reason. Without it, writing simply wouldn't work. Consider that last sentence:

Withoutitwritingsimplywouldn'twork

Space, like silence, gives weight to utterance. It gives the audience time to think, react, and respond. As writers we tend to be afraid of it; this too is unfortunate. Our fear often results in a writing style that is rude and dysfunctional in the extreme: the writer engages in a breathless, self-centered monologue, careening down the page at breakneck speed. He might as well be talking to a brick wall. He frequently is.

Pay attention to silence. Look not only at what you've written but also at what you haven't written. Look not only at the words, sentences, and paragraphs but also at the spaces between them. For there sits your reader, puzzling over the sentence just before and straining to get the gist of the sentence just ahead.

Here's an example of a paragraph in a breathless hurry.

Interest Rate Debt

Since changes in interest rates affect the amount of debt service during the term of the loan, the financing will need to be structured in order to ensure adequate loan payments in the event of such changes. One way to structure the financing is to calculate the loan payments using a high assumed interest rate. Any excess payments could be returned at the end of the loan period, used to prepay principal or credited against future loan payments. A second approach is to specify a two-year interest rate adjustment period. The loan payments will remain fixed for two years and can then be adjusted to cover the new interest rate.

Tough sledding. Not impossible, but certainly not easy. The absence of formatting has turned it into a monolithic block of text: too much information in too little space. Hard to react to, because the writer made no provision for your reactions. There's no room for the reader. Leaving some would seem like common courtesy, but it's a very uncommon one indeed. Why? The writer, data-driven, is writing to himself, not to you.

If we break the paragraph up, we can begin to slow it down.

Interest Rate Debt

Since changes in interest rates affect the amount of debt service during the term of the loan, the financing will need to be structured in order to ensure adequate loan payments in the event of such changes.

Chances are that if you've concentrated on that sentence, your reaction will be something like: "How *should* the financing be structured in order to ensure adequate loan payments?"

The answer comes right after—but in pieces:

One way to structure the financing is to calculate the loan payments using a high assumed interest rate.

A second approach is to specify a two-year interest rate adjustment period.

Why not tell the reader right up front that there are two ways? Why not create some space on the page for the reader to say: "What are they?" And why not give the reader a chance to react to each of them?

An edited, formatted version of this paragraph might begin to look like this:

Interest Rate Debt

Since changes in interest rates affect the amount of debt service during the term of the loan, the financing will need to be structured in order to ensure adequate loan payments in the event of such changes.

There are two ways to ensure adequate debt service.

Reader: "What are they?"

1. Calculate the loan payments using a high assumed interest rate. Any excess payments could be returned at the end of the loan period, used to prepay principal, or credited against future loan payments.

2. Specify a two-year interest rate adjustment period. The loan payments will remain fixed for two years and can then be adjusted to cover the new interest rate.

Notice how the numerals stand in for some of the words ("One way ... A second approach")? Format techniques do precisely this: they substitute visual logic for verbal logic, thereby rendering some of the words superfluous. Think of it this way: By taking away superfluous words, you're making room for essential space.

Digging even deeper into the dialogue, we see that each of the two ways to ensure adequate debt-service coverage itself prompts a question. Here they are, one by one.

1. Calculate the loan payments using a high assumed interest rate.

Reader: "What would happen if the interest rate used was *too* high? What would happen to the excess money?"

See how subtle the dialogue is here? The writer assumes a knowledgeable reader who will expect to see the issue of excess payments addressed on the spot. So what *would* happen to the excess money?

> Any excess payments could be returned at the end of the loan period, used to prepay principal, or credited against future loan payments.

When you get to the end of that tripartite answer, you say to yourself, "Oh, so there are three ways to handle excess payments." Why not give this information to the reader *before* he reads, rather than make him extract it from the text *afterward*? And why not do it visually, using bullets to suggest a set or pattern of alternatives?

> Excess payments could be:
>
> * returned at the end of the loan period;
> * used to prepay principal;
> * credited against future loan payments.

Here's all of point 1, formatted to anticipate, and accommodate, the reader's responses. With all the reactions, spaces, and silences intact.

Interest Rate Debt

> Since changes in interest rates affect the amount of debt service during the term of the loan, the financing will need to be structured in order to ensure adequate loan payments in the event of such changes.
>
> There are two ways to ensure adequate debt service.

1. Calculate the loan payments using a high assumed interest rate. Any excess payments could be:

   - returned at the end of the loan period;
   - used to prepay principal;
   - credited against future loan payments.

So far so good. Now on to point 2, the second way to ensure adequate debt service:

2. Specify a two-year interest rate adjustment period.

Reader: "Why? How will that ensure adequate debt service?"

The loan payments will remain fixed for two years and can then be adjusted to cover the new interest rate.

As you can see, point 2 is simpler than point 1 and does not require the same kind of intricate breakdown. It still, however, anticipates the reader's response. Had the reader responded differently—by wondering, "*How* do we specify it?" or, "Why a *two*-year period?"—the last sentence would have obscured rather than clarified.

Here's the whole revision with the format techniques discussed so far.

Interest Rate Debt

Since changes in interest rates affect the amount of debt service during the term of the loan, the financing will need to be structured in order to ensure adequate loan payments in the event of such changes.

There are two ways to ensure adequate debt service.

1. Calculate the loan payments using a high assumed interest rate. Any excess payments could be:

   - returned at the end of the loan period;
   - used to prepay principal;
   - credited against future loan payments.

2. Specify a two-year interest rate adjustment period. This will mean that the loan payments will remain fixed for two years and can then be adjusted to cover the new interest rate.

This silence-filled, space-filled, interactive revision is good as far as it goes. But there's more to be done. We need to examine the heading to see whether format changes can highlight the dialogue there as well.

EXCAVATING THE MEANING

Consider this phrase:

Interest Rate Debt

Consider the logical relationship between this phrase and the words that follow it.

Interest Rate Debt

Reader: "Huh? What *about* interest rate debt?"

Since changes in interest rates affect the amount of debt service during the term of the loan, the financing will need to be structured in order to ensure adequate loan payments in the event of such changes.

Notice how uninspired this heading is? It doesn't tell you anything. It's little more than a visual and verbal stutter—a kind of mindless, topical announcement that there's more to come. Useful to the writer, but not to the reader, as we can see from the rather primitive, grunt-like response suggested above.

What would have helped the reader? Instead of announcing what's to come, why not synthesize it and present it as the message-driven conclusion?

Ensuring That Loan Payments Cover Debt Service: Two Approaches

This headline excavates the meaning from the paragraph. Imagine your reader as a jaded paleontologist on yet another dig in the vast tundra of corporate prose. With the help of the headline, he easily unearths the dialogue buried on the page, holding it by this question:

What are the two approaches?

The question demands a prescriptive answer, and here it is:

1. **Calculate** the loan payments using a high assumed interest rate.

2. **Specify** a two-year interest rate adjustment period.

Headlines work best when they anticipate, or respond to, the question under discussion. Often that question is the central question in MAPSIQ. At other times it's the question to which a given section or paragraph responds, as it is here. In any case, however, you should try to word your headings so that they elicit more than a descriptive ("What?") response in the reader. They'll be far more effective if they elicit a diagnostic "Why?" or a prescriptive "How?" response.

Boil it down, distill it, make it a useful synthesis. There are many ways to put headings to work here:

- <u>Structuring the Financing: Two Approaches</u>
- <u>How to Ensure Adequate Loan Payments?</u>
- <u>Financing Must Be Structured to Ensure Adequate Loan Payments</u>

Whether phrases, questions, or full sentences, the key is to use headings that prod your reader into participating in the dialogue you have prepared for him. You do this by making sure the headlines you choose convey the essential minimum of your story. Taken together they should present, in effect, an executive summary of the entire document.

When speakers want to create emphasis, they do two things: slow down and speak up. Headlines provide the same logical and vocal emphasis, only they do so visually.

Here's the final product:

Ensuring That Loan Payments Cover Debt Service: Two Approaches

Since changes in interest rates affect the amount of debt service during the term of the loan, the financing will need to be structured in order to ensure adequate loan payments in the event of such changes.

There are two ways to ensure adequate debt service.

1. Calculate the loan payments using a high assumed interest rate. Any excess payments could be:

   • returned at the end of the loan period;
   • used to prepay principal;
   • credited against future loan payments.

2. Specify a two-year interest rate adjustment period. This will mean that the loan payments will remain fixed for two years and can then be adjusted to cover the new interest rate.

Headlines should serve as more than simple markers indicating where to dig; they should highlight the skeleton of what's buried underneath.

Here's an example of how much of the reader's work can be done by the headings. The sample comes from a report on consumer attitudes toward a new product.

Focus Groups

Reader: "Huh? What about them?"

· 72% said they liked the product.

- 75% said they thought the product was reasonably priced.
- 75% said they planned to buy the product.

<u>Focus Group Responses</u>

Reader: "What were the responses?"

- 72% said they liked the product.
- 75% said they thought the product was reasonably priced.
- 75% said they planned to buy the product.

<u>Focus Group Responses Indicate Strong Enthusiasm for the Product</u>

Reader: "They do? Show me."

- 72% said they liked the product.
- 75% said they thought the product was reasonably priced.
- 75% said they planned to buy the product.

Topical headings ("Focus Groups") help the reader concentrate; they help him think hard. Message-driven headings ("Focus Group Responses Indicate Strong Enthusiasm for the Product") help the reader narrow his concentration to think about the right things.

FINDING HIDDEN SYMMETRIES

Writing was born of the urge to get organized. There's evidence to suggest that it evolved first as a memory aid, primarily for record-keeping and accounting purposes.

The earliest form of writing may thus have been the lowly list.

For many of us, making a list is the first step in the tortuous journey from first draft to final document. But there are lists and then there are lists. The ones you jot down for yourself, and the ones you craft—oh so carefully—for your reader. The latter sort is what we're interested in.

There are many ways to present a series of data points: you can number them (1, 2, 3, . . .) outline them (I. A., I. B., I. C. . . . II. A., and so on), or bullet them. Numbering makes sense when you have many points, and when the sequence of those points is part of what you're trying to convey.

Outlining makes sense when convention or complexity dictates: in legal documents, for example, which array a large number of individual, hierarchical pieces of information.

Bullets make sense when the urge to create a pattern is strong; when you wish to reveal hidden symmetries.

Any excess payments could be:

- returned at the end of the loan period;
- used to prepay principal;
- credited against future loan payments.

Note how all three bullets start with the same part of speech, a past participle ("returned . . . used . . . credited")? This is parallelism. The bullets visually anticipate a grammatical and logical pattern. The eye sees the bullets first and is therefore predisposed toward the logical pattern they embody.

Bullets train the reader to see a pattern, and in so doing they act as a kind of mold in which the *meaning* of the pattern is communicated.

To be effective, bullets must do two contradictory things: unite and separate. They must train us to accept their organizing premise, or pattern, while simultaneously indicating what distinguishes each element from the others. Both writer and reader get into trouble if this double purpose is not achieved.

This example, adapted from a hospital job description, illustrates the confusion.

Hospital Administrator

The Hospital Administrator oversees the diagnosis and treatment of human responses to actual or potential problems through such services as liaising with other professionals, teaching, and providing health care supportive to or restorative of life and well-being:

- Assigns and supervises the activities of the nursing staff in the nursing complex.
- Coordinates the 24-hour delivery of nursing care services through supervision and counseling of charge staff.
- Functions as a resource to other hospital staff on the care of the patient.
- Assists and guides nursing staff through patient assessment, care planning, care-plan implementation and evaluation, patient teaching, and documentation.
- Collaborates with other members of the health care team in other departments of the hospital.

- Participates in committees or functions as a resource to ensure quality care and communication in such areas as mini-management, special care, quality assurance, and infection control.

Tough sledding again. Lots of words, lots of bullets, lots of duties.

At first glance, the bullets seem to clarify. They appear to indicate a unity or pattern: a set of nursing duties (each beginning with an active verb: "Assigns . . . Coordinates . . . Functions . . ."). In addition, they break up the text, offering useful slivers of silence for the reader—one sliver between each duty.

On closer inspection, however, they mislead. They do not indicate logical separateness or distinction so much as fuzzy overlap. The white space offers slivers of silence, it is true, but it's the uneasy silence between redundancies, not the confident silence of clarity and definition.

Let's look at the list again. I've numbered the items so we can refer to them more easily.

1. Assigns and supervises the activities of the nursing staff in the nursing complex.
2. Coordinates the 24-hour delivery of nursing care services through supervision and counseling of charge staff.
3. Functions as a resource to other hospital staff on the care of the patient.
4. Assists and guides nursing staff through patient assessment, care planning, care-plan

implementation and evaluation, patient teaching, and documentation.

5. Collaborates with other members of the health care team in other departments of the hospital.

6. Participates in committees or functions as a resource to ensure quality care and communication in such areas as mini-management, special care, quality assurance, and infection control.

Notice how arbitrary they are, in both topic and sequence? Items 1, 2, and 4 have to do with managing staff duties, while 3, 5, and 6 address the common theme of coordination with other functions. I suspect that the culprit, again, is a weary, data-driven writer who has given little thought to the interactive requirements of writing and reading.

How can we turn this arbitrary non-pattern into an organic, logical whole? Regroup the bullets and eliminate the redundancy. Points 1, 2, and 4 become:

Supervises and coordinates the 24-hour delivery of nursing care services in the nursing complex: patient assessment, care planning, care-plan implementation and evaluation, patient teaching, and documentation.

Points 3, 5, and 6 become:

Acts as liaison to other health care teams throughout the hospital; participates in committee work in such

areas as mini-management, special care, quality assurance, and infection control.

I've taken a fairly severe and surgical approach here
to demonstrate that once you peel away the camouflage
of unnecessary words and bullets, the essential points
are two:

The Hospital Administrator manages nurses and
rubs shoulders with other hospital staff.

Having made this discovery, we need to go back to the
heading and introductory statement to see whether they
properly prepare us for this clear double focus:

Hospital Administrator

The Hospital Administrator oversees the diagnosis
and treatment of human responses to actual or potential problems through such services as liaising with
other professionals, teaching, and providing health
care supportive to or restorative of life and well-
being.

The answer is no, and this is precisely the problem. The
topical heading says nothing, and the introductory
statement sheds little light on what follows, simply because it fails to anticipate what's to come in any logical
way. Neither heading nor introduction prompts anything more compelling than "Huh?"
An edited, reformatted version might look like this:

The Hospital Administrator Acts as Supervisor and Liaison

The Hospital Administrator has two distinct roles: supervisor of the entire nursing staff, and liaison between the nursing staff and the rest of the hospital staff.

- As supervisor: coordinates the 24-hour delivery of these nursing care services:
  - patient assessment
  - care planning
  - care-plan implementation and evaluation
  - patient teaching
  - documentation

- As liaison: represents the nursing staff in working with other health care teams throughout the hospital. Member of these and other intradepartmental committees:
  - mini-management
  - special care
  - infection control
  - quality assurance

Once again, these format techniques excavate the logical skeleton buried on the page. I use dashes to indicate yet one more layer, or level, of logic. The intent is to spur another interchange between reader and writer.

It's easy to "please the eye" by throwing a page of bullet points together. It takes skill and forethought to compose a logical group of those points. Three suggestions:

- Use bullets only when there's something to be gained by highlighting the pattern.
- Use bullets only when the grammatical parallels work. If they don't, you may be trying to group elements that don't logically belong together—or that belong in a less rigid format.
- Use bullets only when the individual items are of equal weight and emphasis. If one leads to another and the last one sums up the whole series, then you're highlighting your thinking process rather than the patterned, distilled results of that process.

A cautionary note: Limit the number of bulleted items to between two and six. Any more than that and you'll tax the ability of eye and mind to accept the pattern.

MENDEZ: THE REPRISE

When used wisely, format techniques do much more than reorganize information; they transform it into a fuse that sparks eye, ear, and mind. We have only to examine the Carla Mendez memo from chapter 2 to see how thorough the transformation can be.

Here's the original: the interior monologue of a harried manager. (This is the last time you'll have to look at it. I promise.)

Original

Date: May 6
To: Bob Hartwig
From: Carla Mendez
Subject: May 2 Meeting

Message unstated →

This memo is in response to some questions from last Friday's meeting.

At the conference we need 100 blank manila envelopes, the preprinted material, a sample registration form, and reply cards. We'll also need 75 manila envelopes containing preprinted materials, plus 100 evaluation sheets.

Preconference materials need to be mailed by May 30. Envelopes for this mailing should be the ones with the new design as approved. Preconference material packet includes: preprinted materials, sample registration forms, and reply cards/evaluation sheets.

Randomly presented orders →

Address on mailing envelopes: Sarah will let you know which. Reply cards must fit into mailing envelopes.

Still to come: preconference material, a decision on return address, reply cards, and the conference agenda (we should have about 200 of these at the conference registration table).

It's important that we take Ezra's concerns about price very seriously. As I mentioned, our phone conversation last week underscored how important his input is.

This should wrap it up. I'm sure you can handle everything from here on. I'm leaving tomorrow for a three-week tour of our Asian subsidiaries, followed by some vacation time. See you at the conference.

The Memo Analyzed

Introduction: This memo is in response to some questions from last Friday's meeting.

Question: What questions from last Friday's meeting? (descriptive)

Message: Not stated

Degree of influence achieved: minimal if not negative

- Weak, descriptive Introduction and Question do not prepare reader for prescriptive Message, left unstated.
- Poorly structured body of document consists of randomly presented orders.
- Absence of format techniques all but guarantees that reader will wander off the page.

Here's a revision of the memo at the end of chapter 3.

Revision

Date: May 6
To: Bob Hartwig
From: Carla Mendez
Subject: July 2 Conference

In our May 2 meeting we discussed preparation of July 2 conference materials. I'll be out of the office until then, so here's a recap of what you need to focus on to get the job done:

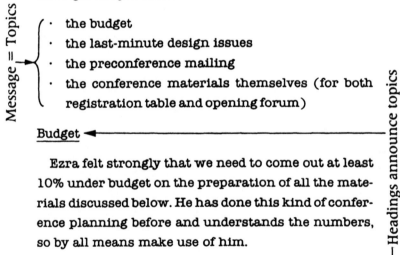

- the budget
- the last-minute design issues
- the preconference mailing
- the conference materials themselves (for both registration table and opening forum)

Budget

Ezra felt strongly that we need to come out at least 10% under budget on the preparation of all the materials discussed below. He has done this kind of conference planning before and understands the numbers, so by all means make use of him.

Design Issues

- reply cards must fit mailing envelopes
- return address on envelopes—Sarah will let you know which. Contact her in a week if she hasn't contacted you.

Message = Topics (left margin annotation)

Headings announce topics (right margin annotation)

Bullets list data (left margin annotation)

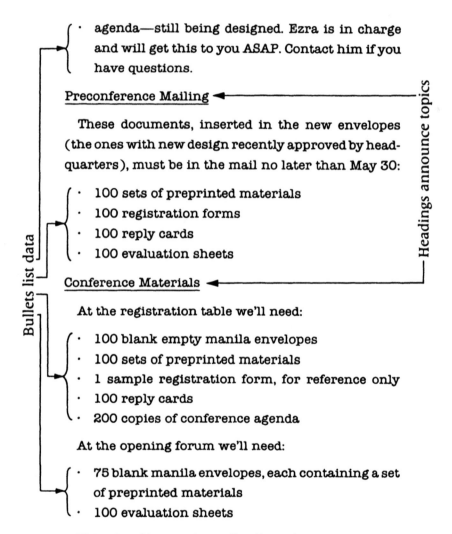

- agenda—still being designed. Ezra is in charge and will get this to you ASAP. Contact him if you have questions.

Preconference Mailing

These documents, inserted in the new envelopes (the ones with new design recently approved by headquarters), must be in the mail no later than May 30:

- 100 sets of preprinted materials
- 100 registration forms
- 100 reply cards
- 100 evaluation sheets

Conference Materials

At the registration table we'll need:

- 100 blank empty manila envelopes
- 100 sets of preprinted materials
- 1 sample registration form, for reference only
- 100 reply cards
- 200 copies of conference agenda

At the opening forum we'll need:

- 75 blank manila envelopes, each containing a set of preprinted materials
- 100 evaluation sheets

This should wrap it up. I will not be easy to reach, so if you have any questions about what needs to get done, ask me before 5:30 this evening. In an emergency, my secretary will be able to phone or fax a message to me, but keep in mind that there will be thirteen time zones between us.

Thanks for your help. See you at the conference.

Bullets list data

Headings announce topics

The Memo Analyzed

Introduction: Here's a recap of what you need to focus on to get the job done.

Question: What do I have to focus on to get the job done? (prescriptive)

Message: Focus on budget, last-minute design issues, preconference mailing, conference materials.

Degree of influence achieved: moderate

- Introduction focuses reader on prescriptive Question "What to do?"
- Body of document consists of sequenced flow of topics, presented in order of importance (political importance, presumably).
- Format techniques reveal descriptive question-answer dialogue:
  - Space provides silence necessary for information to sink in.
  - Headings indicate location of major topics.
  - Bullets list data.

MAPSIQ and format techniques have produced a memo written for the reader, and structured to accommodate the reading process which, once again, consists of imagined dialogue.

But we can improve the quality of that dialogue. In one more version of this memo, we can tighten the relationship between MAPSIQ and format so that the degree of influence is solidly prescriptive throughout.

Final Version

Date: May 6
To: Bob Hartwig
From: Carla Mendez
Subject: Preparation for July 2 Conference—Tasks Remaining

In our May 2 meeting we discussed preparation of July 2 conference materials. I'll be out of the office until then, so here's a recap of what you need to do:

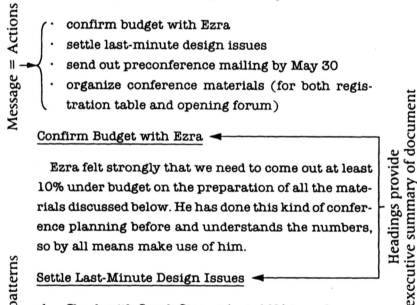

Message = Actions

- confirm budget with Ezra
- settle last-minute design issues
- send out preconference mailing by May 30
- organize conference materials (for both registration table and opening forum)

Confirm Budget with Ezra

Ezra felt strongly that we need to come out at least 10% under budget on the preparation of all the materials discussed below. He has done this kind of conference planning before and understands the numbers, so by all means make use of him.

Settle Last-Minute Design Issues

- Check with Sarah Strang (ext. 441) to make sure that reply cards will fit into mailing envelopes, and to confirm correct return address on envelopes. Contact her in a week if she hasn't contacted you.
- Confer with Ezra about the convention agenda, still being designed.

Bullets indicate logical patterns

Headings provide executive summary of document

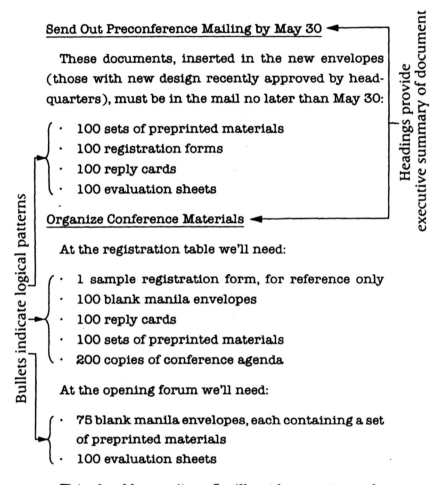

Send Out Preconference Mailing by May 30

These documents, inserted in the new envelopes (those with new design recently approved by headquarters), must be in the mail no later than May 30:

- 100 sets of preprinted materials
- 100 registration forms
- 100 reply cards
- 100 evaluation sheets

Organize Conference Materials

At the registration table we'll need:

- 1 sample registration form, for reference only
- 100 blank manila envelopes
- 100 reply cards
- 100 sets of preprinted materials
- 200 copies of conference agenda

At the opening forum we'll need:

- 75 blank manila envelopes, each containing a set of preprinted materials
- 100 evaluation sheets

Bullets indicate logical patterns

Headings provide executive summary of document

This should wrap it up. I will not be easy to reach, so if you have any questions about what needs to get done, ask me before 5:30 this evening. In an emergency, my secretary will be able to phone or fax a message to me, but keep in mind that there will be thirteen time zones between us.

Thanks for your help. See you at the conference.

The Memo Analyzed

Introduction: Here's a recap of what you need to do.

Question: What do I have to do? (prescriptive)

Message: Confirm budget with Ezra, settle last-minute design issues, send out preconference mailing, organize conference materials.

Degree of influence achieved: optimal

- Introduction, Question, and Message focus reader on *specific actions* rather than general themes.
- Body of document consists of sequenced flow of recommendations, presented in order of importance (political importance, presumably).
- Format techniques spark a tighter, more focused question-answer dialogue:

  — Space provides silence necessary for reader to react.
  — Headings state actions directly; taken together, they are an executive summary of document.
  — Bullets have been resequenced and regrouped to indicate logical patterns and relationships.

In the final version, the manager's clarity catalyzes the employee into action. That clarity is illustrated in the power of the dialogue revealed in the memo's structure and tone.

THE WRITER'S PROGRESS

Here are the subject headings for all three versions of the Mendez memo:

Original: May 2 Meeting
Revision: July 2 Conference
Final Version: Preparation for July 2 Conference—
                 Tasks Remaining

Each of them is true to its word; each accurately prepares the reader for what's to come.

Examined together, they tell the entire story of how writers think. They illustrate the shift from monologue to dialogue. They mark the progress from data-driven, internally focused thought to reader-driven, externally focused communication. Or to put it another way: Without some sort of intervention, the writer generally starts descriptively and ends diagnostically or prescriptively.

Writing is a journey, as we have said. This is fine except for one problem. In business you travel alone. You can't expect the reader to go along with you. The reader isn't really interested in the journey—it's the destination that matters.

With practice the journey gets shorter and quicker. MAPSIQ can help you decide where you're going and how best to get there. Format techniques help too. They can show you what the destination looks like before you arrive, so that you'll recognize it. They help you visualize the writer-reader dialogue so that you can put it on the page. If you can see it in your mind you can write it down.

A suggestion: Think about format when you write, not just when you edit. Think about format when you think about MAPSIQ, and particularly when you wrestle with Question and Message. Put the format to work in your head before you put it to work on paper. Put it to work for yourself before you put it to work for the reader. Make the dialogue as vivid as you can.

CHAPTER SIX

Editing: The Politics

Ask managers about the hardest parts of their job and inevitably they mention the difficulties of managing difficult people. How to keep them focused? How to keep them motivated? How to make sure they contribute?

When it comes to writing and editing in the corporate environment, we are *all* difficult people.

.   .   .

You are one of five writers involved in putting together a huge strategic plan for your division. You know the other writers only slightly. You have two weeks to complete the project. At the kickoff meeting it becomes clear that everyone has a different view of what the document should say and how it should say it. One favors a telephone-book approach, with every scrap of data included. Another wants the document as short as possible. Another wants to use as many charts and graphs as possible. Another declares herself far too busy to do any writing whatsoever. There are too many cooks for this soup, and not one of them has a recipe. This strikes you as a nifty analogy and you're about to share it, but you bite your tongue. You have no intention of becoming the master chef.

.   .   .

You've asked three staff members to collaborate on an article for a national trade journal. It's to be published under your name (your first byline). You have never written anything like this before, and you charge your team to "get some thoughts on paper." They come back with a draft, which looks, sounds, and reads too much like a draft to give you any confidence that they're getting anywhere. You send them off to try another approach. They come back a few days later. In the interim you have reworked the first draft. As they enter your office to discuss draft 2, you launch in on draft 1. Two of your staff stare out the window, and the third doodles on the pad she brought with her. You ask for another version in a day or two. When they return with draft 3, you hand out copies of the version you've been working on and begin to discuss its merits. No one will look you in the eye, and no one says anything. You sense that something is profoundly wrong.

.   .   .

Your Ph.D. dissertation on fractals was the high point of your writing life. You left the hallowed halls of academe three years ago to muck about in the muddy corridors of commerce. Your writing exudes a certain arrogance that you perceive as a high order of precision. Those who don't like the way you write simply don't understand what good writing is, you conclude. What you find puzzling is that other people—people whose writing is clearly inferior to yours—fail to appreciate the perspective and knowledge you bring to the editing process. More often than not, your suggestions fall on deaf ears.

What you have never realized is that you cannot edit because you cannot *be edited*.

.   .   .

The management dimension of writing is nowhere more vivid than in the editing process. For it is here, working with writers to revise their documents and refine their thinking, that you can exert the greatest leverage in developing colleagues and staff.

Editing your own work is like trying to give yourself a haircut without a mirror when deep down you really think you look fine the way you are. Tackling someone else's work is easier in a way. Your critical faculties are far more energetically deployed. This isn't going to hurt *you*, after all. But what happens when you have to edit not only the writing but the writer too? Editing someone else's writing from the glorious sanctuary of your office or kitchen table is not the same as confronting the writer and convincing him that you know better than he does.

The success of that confrontation is grounded in your ability to treat the writer, the writing process, and the revision process with respect. Some of the skills involved are editorial, but unless they're part of an effective managerial dialogue you'll never have the chance to put them to work.

Editing sessions are much like performance reviews. The stakes are high; the data is often soft and subjective. As a result, the interpersonal dynamic is fragile.

Insecure writers generally make insecure editors. As I mentioned in chapter 1, the roots of insecurity run deep—and extend their subterranean grip on the editing process too. The way you edit is heavily influenced by the way you have been edited. Most people can report a run-in with at least one of these three editorial types:

1. the teacher: "There's a right way and a wrong way, and you're doing it the wrong way. Let me show you the right way."
2. the slave driver: "Do it this way or else."
3. the visionary: "I'll know it's the way I want it when I see it the way I want it."

None of these editorial styles works. The reason? They're bad management. They're bad management because they create adversarial relationships, not collaborative ones. They create adversarial relationships because they assume that the "managing editor" is always right, and that the writer is there solely to do the manager's bidding. All three of these styles, in other words, boil down to one: *Do it my way.*

This chapter examines the editing process in all its corporate complexity. By "corporate complexity" I mean politics. In the next chapter I show how to tackle the words on the page; in this chapter I show how to tackle the people who write them. I focus first on the management skills involved, since those are the ones most frequently ignored.

THE TUG-OF-WAR

I worked once with an urbane, sophisticated consultant. I was the editor, he the edited. This was a role he was clearly uncomfortable with, and I had the impression that he would have preferred to sit on my side of the table. Which he tried to do, figuratively speaking, more than once during our ninety-minute session. We talked. We even sparred. Eventually we began to examine a document that he had written. Every comment I made was perceived as an assault on the purity of his prose. After each of my remarks he counterattacked with passion and eloquence.

This writer is the embodiment of a particular species of corporate writer for whom the reader/editor is the enemy: the Other. Writing is a form of combat. The document is the Holy Grail, whose honor must be defended against the infidel: the reader who challenges its integrity by suggesting changes.

It became clear that we were engaged not in a dialogue but in a battle: a tug-of-war with the document between us. There was, of course, something else between us: the writer's vulnerability. *Criticize this document and you criticize me.*

Vulnerability must be respected. It's part of us all, regardless of how skilled or talented we are—and regardless of how confident we seem. Here is one writer's description of how it felt to submit drafts to senior management:

> I sometimes thought it was like sending a beautiful newborn fawn out into the jagged wilderness where the grosser animals would pierce its tender flesh and render mortal wounds. But perhaps I understate.*

---

* Peggy Noonan, *What I Saw at the Revolution* (New York: Random House, 1990), p. 76.

But back to the consultant. I questioned the clarity of one particular sentence:

> While succession planning is certainly an important consideration for Proctor Inc., we do not feel that it has a direct bearing on the analysis.

I pointed out that the reader might be confused here. It sounded as if the sentence contained a contradiction: Succession planning is important, but it's not important. I said that the supporting idea, "While succession planning is certainly an important consideration for Proctor Inc.," might be the culprit.

I suggested that the consultant test the logic of the sentence by reversing its two parts, so that the sentence would start with the main idea, "We do not feel that it has a direct bearing on the analysis." I proposed this method as a way to figure out which part of the sentence contained the major message. So the sentence

> While succession planning is certainly an important consideration for Proctor Inc., we do not feel that it has a direct bearing on the analysis.

became

> We do not feel that succession planning has a direct bearing on the analysis, even though it is important.

The consultant stopped me: "No, wait—you're wrong. That's not what it says. What the sentence says is, 'While Proctor Inc. may think that succession planning is important to the analysis, we do not.' "

"So what you mean to convey is the distinction between your views and Proctor Inc.'s views on the importance of succession planning to the analysis?" He nodded.

"That's not the only way to read this sentence," I said. "I've read it ten times in the past half-hour, and this is the first time I've understood what you meant to convey: not 'Succession planning is important,' but 'Proctor Inc. thinks succession planning is important to the analysis, and we don't.' Who's right? Me? You? The next reader?"

He was silent for a long minute. "I see what you're driving at," he said slowly. "You're saying that the sentence I wrote is *itself* an interpretation—my interpretation of what I intended to say—and that the reader can do nothing but interpret my interpretation."

I sensed a fundamental shift. The shift that occurs when the writer is himself on the line, forced to look at his writing from the reader's perspective and admit that no, it isn't clear. I've witnessed it thousands of times. There is no more jolting epiphany in a writer's life, and none more useful; for with it comes the realization that meaning does not reside in the document, static and unchanging. Meaning visits the document with each reader and each reading. When all is said and read, it's the reader, not the writer, who ultimately judges the document's meaning and utility.

All the editorial skill in the world won't come to a hill of beans unless you can convert the writer to the reader's vantage point. You need to be coach and collaborator, not critic. You need to be a mentor as well as a manager. You need to create and sustain a dialogue with the writer.

YOU REPRESENT THE READER

As a manager, the hardest task you face is bringing the writer around to this way of thinking, showing him that meaning depends on the reader, not just the document (or the writer). Your success in doing so will mean that you have lifted a huge burden from the writer's shoulders—the burden of producing a "perfect" memo or report. And with this burden lifted, the writer will actually be able to hear what you have to say, since he will no longer be waiting tensely for the grade to be given, for the final judgment to be rendered regarding his intelligence or skill.

You function as a bridge, an intermediary between writer and reader. This means becoming the reader from time to time, but it also means helping the writer become the reader. Your goal: to teach the writer to hop back and forth between his head and the reader's, to show him how to enhance the dialogue by seeing the differences between his job (thoughts into words) and the reader's (words into thoughts).

Your job, in sum, is to represent the reader. I mean "represent" in two senses of the word: (1) "symbolize" or "stand in for," and (2) "defend," the way a lawyer defends a client. In the first instance, you "play" reader. You adopt the biases, interests, and agendas of the reader so that the writer can have the benefit of a dress rehearsal, so to speak. In the second instance, you help the writer understand how difficult the reading process really is. You point out all the places in the document where the reader can go wrong.

"I SEE WHAT YOU'RE DRIVING AT"

Many professions adopt specific communications styles suited to their purposes; lawyers, doctors, clergy, and counselors have all developed techniques for interacting successfully with their clientele.

Here's an example of how important it is to have such a style. The editor is describing the process of editing "up," that delicate task of giving feedback to those who are senior and thus more powerful.

> I always wanted to handle these people with a lovely finesse, a marvelous grace. I wanted to do it the way Gerald Murphy did when he told the off-key singer, "Ah yes, and now you must rest your lovely vocal chords." But because I always felt threatened . . . I would sputter. "I'm sorry," I'd say, "but that just doesn't work. It's not quite right. Well, it just doesn't. It's just not—oh look, it's just dumb, I'm sorry it's dumb but it is, it's shit."*

How can you get through to the writer and keep his ego intact—while maintaining your own integrity and professionalism? Here are six management techniques that help:

---

* Noonan, p. 77.

1. Map out the writing tasks before the writing begins.
2. Edit in person, not just on paper.
3. Use MAPSIQ to structure the discussion.
4. Take the telescopic view before the microscopic.
5. Keep your remarks reader-based, not writer-based.
6. Know your idiosyncrasies; be prepared to negotiate.

These will do great things for the writer and the document. They'll also do great things for you: you'll be a better editor, a better manager, and a better mentor.

1. Map out the writing tasks before the writing begins.

Before you let your staff loose on a writing project, give them as much management guidance as you can.

- Use MAPSIQ as a project management tool. Call a meeting to discuss Message, Audience, Purpose, Situation, Introduction, and Question, in order to instill a common understanding of where the project is headed.
- Use a flip chart to sketch a mock-up of the document so that the writers can visualize the end result and work toward it more confidently.

  — Discuss how long you think the document should be.
  — Discuss the sequence, flow, and length of the subsections.

— Try out a couple of headlines to show your staff how to synthesize the messages.
— Sketch one or two exhibits, complete with titles, to show the writers what data they need to collect and what they should then do with it.

- Make it clear that you're available for consultation as writers begin to work on their drafts.
- Schedule additional progress meetings as appropriate.

The time you spend at the front end will be amply compensated for as you reach the deadline. The writers start stronger and move faster. When you reach the editing stage, you do so collectively—and all the writers share the same understanding of what's happening. The most effective managers I know are those who bring project management skills to the writing process.

2. Edit in person, not just on paper.

By all means annotate the draft you have, suggesting changes; but sit down with the writer and discuss the document as well. Your presence will help make several things possible.

First, it will make the reader and the act of reading vivid to the writer. You can't represent the reader in the two ways I described above—symbolize his purpose and defend his plight—without becoming real to the writer. You can't stand in for the reader in absentia; and you certainly can't defend the reader's point of view unless you're there to talk about what that point of view might be. The reader will not materialize in any constructive way unless you do.

Second, your presence will keep the writer from regressing. If you take the easy way out and simply scribble in the margins, you risk sending the writer right back to sixth grade. Right back to Sister Mary, to red pen in the margins, to memories of "Awk.," "Sp.," and "Unclear." Regardless of how good your intentions may be, I will guarantee that a note like this:

> This needs work. I've written some suggestions in the margins. Why don't you try another draft and come back later.

stapled to the draft, will be far less successful than an actual conversation.

In annotating the document, do what you can to keep the text—and the writer's confidence—intact.

- Use pencil, not pen.
- Frame your remarks as comments or questions to the writer, using the margins or posted notes. Do not write corrections on top of the text itself.
- Use a separate sheet for your own thoughts and scribbles.

Your presence does more than invoke the reader and build confidence. It also gives you the chance to model a successful dialogue about a business problem, so that your employees learn the approach you take and the way you like to think. You are therefore teaching coaching skills while simultaneously practicing them yourself. The leverage you gain here is as much managerial as editorial.

3. Use MAPSIQ to structure the discussion.

Before you sit down with the writer, sit down with the document and MAPSIQ. Use MAPSIQ to take the pulse of the document, just as you use it to take the pulse of the writers when you launch the writing project.

How faithfully does the draft reflect that initial MAPSIQ? Has the writer addressed all the audiences for this document? Has he carefully thought through the purposes? Does he have a clear sense of what needs to happen next? Does the document address the right question? Does it answer it fully? Chances are your perspective on Audience, Purpose, Situation, and Question will add much to the discussion, if you've prepared for the meeting by assessing the document along these lines.

Here's an example of how *not* to lead the discussion. E is the editor; W the writer.

E: I didn't understand what you were driving at.

W: [*Bristling but trying not to sound defensive*] Perhaps I wasn't clear. . . . What I was saying is that the modeling approach we used was inadequate.

E: Why didn't you say that?

W: I did—it's all throughout the document!

E: Where? I didn't catch it.

W: It's here on page four, and I say it again on page seven—at the bottom.

E: Well, anyway, the committee doesn't care about the modeling approach. They want to hear about results, not how we got them.

W: This memo isn't about results.

E: Yes, I know. That's what I'm saying.

W: [*Speaking softly so as not to lose her temper*] When you asked me to write this memo, you told me to focus on how effective the modeling approach was. So that's what I did.

E: Well, the committee wants to hear about results. Please take this memo and beef up the discussion about the results.

The coach has turned critic. There's plenty going wrong here: the accusatory tone, the adversarial I-versus-you confrontation—a tug-of-war, with the document in the middle. The editor sounds impatient and irritable, not to mention ill prepared.

It becomes obvious that the writing project was launched in a most haphazard way, without any kind of MAPSIQ preparation by editor or writer. As a result, this review meeting fizzles out. It might have remained airborne had the editor introduced a MAPSIQ discussion here, but that didn't happen. So the writer takes the heat for the editor's mismanagement.

Here's a better way:

E: You've done a nice job of explaining the modeling problems, but the operations committee is far more interested in the solutions. Why don't you try another draft, highlighting the solutions?

This approach takes the adversarial sting out, but it still falls short in that it provides no specific guidance. Far too often managerial feedback is vague and unspecific. How easy will it be for the writer to "highlight the solutions"?

Better still:

> E: You've got a terrific diagnostic document here—you spell out the problems with the modeling approach clearly and logically. But I know the operations committee wants a prescriptive report: they want the recommendations. Can you pose the central question as a "How to fix?" Why not briefly mention the problems in the intro, pose the "How to fix?" question, and then have each recommendation become a section?

The editor has pinpointed both what's right and what's wrong with the document. He has invoked the reader as the determinant of Purpose and Question—there's nothing personal about this assessment. Moreover, MAPSIQ has brought the writer gently back to the business landscape so that he is forced to think about the forest rather than the trees.

The editor has made concrete suggestions; they are posed as questions so as not to threaten the writer, and they are specific enough that the writer can walk back to his office visualizing the changes he needs to make.

But most important, the writer has learned something about how the manager thinks and how he manages. The benefits are two. First, as the writer develops, he'll require less and less supervision, so that both writer and manager can be more productive. And second, both will have increased their own power by putting it to work in other people.

4. Take the telescopic view before the microscopic.

The single most frequently voiced frustration among business writers is that editors do more harm than good. Indeed, corporate America is full of writers so cowed by the capriciousness with which management wields its red pencil that it's a wonder anyone ever has the courage to produce a first draft.

The editor begins:

> E: This paragraph struck me as a bit vague. I don't know what you're saying here.
> W: Well, as you can see from the first sentence [*trying to sound tension-free*], I'm talking about the new floor plan.
> E: Yes, but you use the word "allocation" here. A better word would be "configuration." I had an English teacher once who ... [*Editor drones on, writer tunes out.*]

This manager is committing the biggest editorial sin of all: starting small, taking issue with the specifics, the actual words on the page. He does so, presumably, because it's easier to talk about a word or a sentence in isolation than to tackle the structure or sense of an entire document. He ought to be forgiven for this, but he never is.

The upshot, of course, is an editorial tug-of-war. The writer bears a legitimate grudge: How dare the editor toy with the words before demonstrating any understanding of the audience, the purpose, and the message?

The wiser approach is to tackle the editing process in

stages. It makes sense to examine the material from three different perspectives: the document level, the component level, and the sentence level. At each level ask yourself two questions: What is the major message? Where is it?

MAPSIQ will take you directly to Level I—the document level. Once you've established what the message is and where it's located, you've determined what kind of logical structure the document has. This is essential information to have before proceeding to Level II, the component level.

Depending on the length and complexity of the document, a Level II edit will focus on chapters, sections, or paragraphs. Again, the same two questions apply: What's the major message in this paragraph or section? *Where* is it? In addition, you should ask yourself: Is the message clear? Should it be moved up or highlighted in some way? Does it clearly link back to the central question the document addresses? If not, how can I make it do so?

Once you've done a thorough Level II edit, and only then, are you ready to tackle Level III: sentence-level editing. Again, a negative and all too realistic illustration.

E: I read it over last night. Basically, it's okay. But it's kind of wordy, don't you think?

W: I don't think so. . . . You asked me to keep it under five pages, and I did.

E: I don't know, it seems like it kind of rambles. Try tightening it up a bit.

W: [*Puzzled*] Are you saying it's too long?

E: No . . . not really. I don't know, it just isn't very punchy. Why don't you try making it a bit more punchy?

W: [*Bewildered*] Okay . . .

These remarks *sound* like comments about the sentences; perhaps the document does ramble. I suspect, however, that a Level I edit that clearly identified the major message and repositioned it at the beginning of the document would have gone a long way toward reducing the wordiness. In the next chapter I'll discuss what to look for in sentence-level editing. But suffice it to say that when editing in person, you're better off working from the big picture first.

Speaking of working from the big picture: When you point out errors in spelling, grammar, punctuation, and usage, you're working from the smallest picture imaginable. Granted, these are the first things you spot when you edit, but they should be the *last* things on your agenda. The reason, of course, is that they're the last things on the *writer's* agenda.

Use forbearance. The mechanical errors must be addressed; indeed, they often provide clues to more serious flaws of logic and structure. But they can wait until you've managed to convince the writer that you've got a solid grasp of his intentions. Nothing sets a writer more on edge than nitpicky corrections undertaken before, or instead of, insightful editing. The management parallel here is striking: whenever you give feedback, do so in the way that will make it easiest for the employee to accept—not easiest for you to prepare.

Incidentally, this is another reason why editing someone's work on paper alone is so risky. The writer sees a jumble of corrections with absolutely no hierarchy or priority. The ghost of Sister Mary stalks the page.

5. Keep your remarks reader-based, not writer-based.

Since the entire framework for planning and writing the document is based on MAPSIQ, a reader-based approach, it makes sense to sustain this focus all the way through to the editing process. Invoke the reader and you stand a good chance of sustaining the writer through the revisions.

Here are some bad—and better—examples.

Scenario 1
Bad

You need to change the tone—this is much too direct.

Better

I know that Robin intends to send this over to the legal department after she's seen it. They usually take a very conservative stance, and I suspect they'll ship this right back to us and tell us it's too direct. What can we do to keep the message intact but make it sound less threatening?

Scenario 2
Bad

This is much too long. It took you twenty pages to get to the main part of your argument, and by then I'd lost all interest.

Better

The reader will probably want to know right at the beginning why you think the rate increase is warranted.

Not "I," but "the reader." You represent the reader.

6. Know your idiosyncrasies; be prepared to negotiate.

All of us have the urge to leave our mark. When you sit down with a writer, it's good to remember the "Rule of Thirds," which goes something like this: Editorial remarks fall into three categories—essential, advisable, and arbitrary. It's important to know which remarks fall into which category, so that you have some negotiating room.

It's often true, for example, that comments about the writer's choice of words reflect little more than the editor's stylistic whims. How foolish it would be, then, to begin a discussion here, or do anything else that would once again set up an editorial tug-of-war.

How to distinguish essential changes from advisable changes, or advisable from arbitrary? The reader and MAPSIQ must be the guides. Given Audience, Purpose, and Situation, what must be changed? What would be *nice* to change? The editor may need to give a little, in order to let the writer keep control over some of the review process.

It's also possible, of course, that the writer knows best. If so, he needs to be able to demonstrate that superior knowledge—just as the editor must do so by invoking the reader and the act of reading. If you've used MAPSIQ throughout the entire planning, writing, and revision process, both you and the writer can discuss the document logically and without acrimony. The reason is that you've established a formal mechanism for communicating, for the give-and-take so essential to the management dialogue.

THE MANAGING EDITOR

As a managing editor, you sit on either a powder keg or a gold mine, depending on how well you assess, develop, and exploit the writing skills of your staff.

The managing editor is a mentor, and the potential for leverage is enormous. You can set the standards you want and can work, visibly, to achieve them. You can create a mechanism for your staff to model both your output and your behavior. You can create an environment conducive to teamwork and feedback. You can develop the coaching skills of your staff and provide them a way to develop not only their skills but also the skills of the people who report to them. Editing is quality control—of the process, the product, and the people.

The best way to help your staff become better writers is to teach them how to become better editors. Teach them by becoming a better editor yourself.

CHAPTER SEVEN

Editing: The Tools

In the last chapter I talked about people. In this chapter I talk about words, whether your own or someone else's.

Editors who start at the word level do so at their peril, as I mentioned in chapter 6. If you're editing someone else's writing, you may damage not only your relationship with the writer, but the document as well. The reason is that you risk straying off the writer's path onto one of your own creation. If you're editing your own writing, you may circle endlessly. It's only when you've taken the measure of a document's logic and structure that you're fully positioned to tackle the logic of individual sentences. There's always a link between them, but that link may not be clear. Your job is to clarify it.

Below is a paragraph that needs a good edit. You've seen it before—I've taken it from chapter 1.

For all the reasons outlined above, it seems to be prudent to find a solution to the pricing problem as soon as is humanly possible. Also, it is the responsibility of this department to be closely allied with the marketing and the purchasing departments. Together, these three groups should be systematically reviewing all the viable pricing options in order to clearly identify the one set of parameters that is most accurate in terms of the profitability objectives that were established by the planning committee at the last strategy offsite.

The revision, also from the first chapter, looks like this:

We need to solve the pricing problem immediately. This department will spend the next week working with the marketing and purchasing departments. Our objective: to find the best pricing structure, given the profitability objectives from the last strategy meeting.

Here are the seven techniques I used to create the revision:

1. Use a human subject and a strong verb whenever possible.
2. Keep the subject and verb close together.
3. Shorten sentences.
4. Consider alternatives to "is."
5. Avoid plural nouns.
6. Beware faulty connective tissue.
7. Edit out loud.

Let's take a look at each one.

1. Use a human subject and a strong verb whenever possible.

The biggest change in the revision is that the manager puts himself back on the page. The sentence

For all the reasons outlined above, it seems to be prudent to find a solution to the pricing problem as soon as is humanly possible.

becomes

We need to solve the pricing problem immediately.

Substituting "we" for "it" lays the groundwork for every other change in the paragraph. Using a human subject permitted—indeed, forced—the use of a strong verb "need" in place of the anemic "seems to be prudent."

This is very often what happens to verbs when they have human subjects: they become real; they actually do something.

If you feel uncomfortable using a person's name or a pronoun ("I," "you," "he," "she," "they"), you can still reveal some humanity by using the company or department name. In the second sentence, for example, "Also, it is the responsibility of this department to be closely allied with the marketing and the purchasing departments" became "This department will spend the next few weeks working with the marketing and purchasing departments." The human subject ("this department") forced a strong verb ("will spend").

2. Keep the subject and verb close together.

Using a human subject also forced the verb to go back where it belongs: close to the subject. When the verb wanders too far from the subject, the energy of the sentence is dissipated to an alarming degree. The punch of the English language comes from the punch of subject and verb together.

> This department will spend the next week working
> with the marketing and purchasing departments.

3. Shorten sentences.

Once you've managed to concentrate the energy of
the sentence in one place, you should keep it there.
You'll be able to do so if you keep your sentences reasonably short; one major idea and one supporting idea
is a good benchmark.

Here's a sentence from the original:

> Together, these three groups should be systematically
> reviewing all the viable pricing options in order to
> clearly identify the one set of parameters that is most
> accurate in terms of the profitability objectives that
> were established by the planning committee at the
> last strategy offsite.

And here's the revision, in which one long sentence
becomes two shorter ones:

> This department will spend the next week working
> with the marketing and purchasing departments.

> Our objective: to find the best pricing structure, given
> the profitability objectives from the last strategy
> meeting.

Where to break? There's no easy answer. Some say to
break where you breathe, that is, where you instinc-
tively feel the need to pause. Some say to break where
the commas are. (With any luck, the commas mark the
places where you might need to breathe.) My sugges-

tion: Think of the reader, and break where the logic tells you to.

4. Consider alternatives to "is."

The last sentence I wrote ("My suggestion: Think of the reader, and break where the logic tells you to") demonstrates the fourth technique. I could have written: "My suggestion *is* to think of the reader, and break where the logic tells you to," but I didn't. I made a choice to stay away from the verb "to be." It's the weakest, most lackluster verb we have, and yet it's the one we use most often. I've highlighted it in the sample paragraph:

> For all the reasons outlined above, it seems **to be** prudent to find a solution to the pricing problem as soon as **is** humanly possible. Also, it **is** the responsibility of this department **to be** closely allied with the marketing and the purchasing departments. Together, these three groups should **be** systematically reviewing all the viable pricing options in order to clearly identify the one set of parameters that **is** most accurate in terms of the profitability objectives that **were** established by the planning committee at the last strategy offsite.

Here's the revision:

> We need to solve the pricing problem immediately. This department will spend the next week working with the marketing and purchasing departments. Our objective: to find the best pricing structure, given the profitability objectives from the last strategy meeting.

Seven have been reduced to none. Not bad. The important thing, however, is not how many there are, but how much damage they do to the logic—and the leverage—of the sentences in which they occur. Verbs convey action, prescription. The verb "is" does not; it conveys stasis and description. The more "to be" verbs in a given sentence or paragraph, the more descriptive that sentence or paragraph will be.

If you don't believe me, reread the original paragraph—do you sense that anything is actually going to get done?

5. Avoid plural nouns.

And speaking of description: There is no more deadly combination than "to be" verbs and plural nouns:

> For all the **reasons** outlined above, it seems to be prudent to find a solution to the pricing problem as soon as is humanly possible. Also, it is the responsibility of this department to be closely allied with the marketing and the purchasing **departments**. Together, these three **groups** should be systematically reviewing all the viable pricing **options** in order to clearly identify the one set of **parameters** that is most accurate in terms of the profitability **objectives** that were established by the planning committee at the last strategy offsite.

See what a faint perspective they create? The manager seems suspended in midair, far above the specifics. The elevated view sounds vaguely authoritative until you begin to examine the paragraph a bit closer, at which point it simply sounds vague.

The revision, by contrast, fairly sparkles with precision:

> We need to solve the pricing problem immediately. This department will spend the next week working with the marketing and purchasing departments. Our objective: to find the best pricing structure, given the profitability objectives from the last strategy meeting.

6. Beware faulty connective tissue.

The writer-manager's challenge, as we have seen, is to create and sustain a conversation with the reader. The dialogue must always focus out toward the audience, never in toward the writer. Examining the connective tissue can help editors identify where dialogue slips back into monologue. Consider these sentences:

> For all the reasons outlined above, it seems to be prudent to find a solution to the pricing problem as soon as is humanly possible. **Also**, it is the responsibility of this department to be closely allied with the marketing and the purchasing departments.

Why "also"? It's a jarring cue for the reader, since it signals a kind of logical parity between the two sentences—a parity not borne out by the thrust of the paragraph.

I suspect that this "also" is not meant for the reader at

all, but rather for the writer as he begins to think about how he wants to write this paragraph ("First I'll talk about the need to find a solution. . . . Then I'll talk about the department working in conjunction with other departments. . . .").

Beware faulty connective tissue: "also," "in addition," "therefore," "thus," "in summary," "in conclusion," and so on. These are helpful if the writer is fully engaged in a dialogue with the reader. They wreak havoc when they're remarks left over from the writer's monologue.

7. Edit out loud.

All the techniques discussed so far have one aim: to make reading and writing easier so that the dialogue on paper fully supports the managerial one. The key is to restore to our writing the sounds and rhythms of human speech. We can do so by producing those sounds and rhythms with our own voices.

Reading the document over silently isn't enough. Asking someone else to read it over silently isn't enough either. You need to hear your words—their heft and emphasis—with the texture and inflection of a real voice, not just an imagined one.

Read your words aloud. Better yet, turn your words over to someone else and ask him to read your words aloud to *you.*

You'll hear far more this way than you ever thought imaginable. You'll hear another voice—and watch another thinker—try to interact with your thoughts. You'll instantly detect fault lines in logic. And you'll instantly be convinced that no, it isn't as clear as you thought it was.

But most important, you'll have the heady opportunity to eavesdrop on the writer-reader dialogue as it takes place. What better way to learn how to listen to your reader?

Conclusion

A senior manager in a financial services firm called me in to work with a brilliant young associate. We met at the appointed hour. He sat down across the table from me, smiled affably, and said, "Look. I don't want to waste your time. I don't need a writing course. I don't have time for a writing course. I already know how to write."

I said nothing.

"I'm very conceptual," he continued. "I know my analytical strengths. I'm a born communicator. There really isn't anything you can do for me."

Still I kept quiet.

He paused. "There is one thing, though, that I'd be interested in knowing," he said slowly. He took a sheet of paper off a pad. "It would help my learning curve enormously. . . ." As he talked, he sketched. I glanced down and saw:

$$+ \quad - \quad \times \quad \% \quad =$$

"All I want are the verbal equivalents," he said. "Now *that* would be useful."

Since then I've thought a lot about that conversation. What did he want from me? Something that neither I nor anyone else could provide: a set of rules that would render his writing completely free of ambiguity. As free from ambiguity as

$$+ \quad - \quad \times \quad \% \quad =$$

I answered him in this way. I stated that no such equivalents existed. I declared that words, unlike mathematical symbols, are drenched in ambiguity. They're drenched in ambiguity because people are. I suggested that the key to writing well was to learn how to manage this ambiguity so that we are more or less in control of it—and our readers.

This book is about managing ambiguity in the corporate world. It's no easy task, for the corporate world has a low tolerance for ambiguity; after all, it's a place where numbers rule supreme.

Managers know this better than anyone. Make the numbers—but grow the people. Can't do both? Well, make the numbers.

We *must* do both. We must develop the people *and* make the numbers. How? By exploiting the links among thinking, communicating, and managing.

The more clearly you think, the better you write. The better you write, the more effectively you communicate. The more effectively you communicate, the more successfully you manage.

These are the skills that develop people and make the numbers: the skills that turn good managers into superior ones, and superior managers into executives. There are many other skills, but none more important than your ability to manage the ambiguity of words, ideas, and people.

Sources

Flower, Linda. *Problem-Solving Strategies for Writing.* New York: Harcourt Brace Jovanovich, 1981.

Minto, Barbara. *The Pyramid Principle.* London: Minto International Inc., 1981.

Noonan, Peggy. *What I Saw at the Revolution.* New York: Random House, 1990.

Ong, Walter J. *Orality & Literacy: The Technologizing of the Word.* London and New York: Methuen, 1982.

Slobin, Daniel Isaac. *Psycholinguistics*, Second Edition. Glenview, Illinois: Scott Foresman, 1979.

Steiner, George. *Real Presences.* Chicago: University of Chicago Press, 1989.

Todorov, Tzvetan. *Mikhail Bakhtin: The Dialogical Principle.* Translated by Wlad Godzich. Theory and History of Literature, volume 13. Minneapolis: University of Minnesota Press, 1984.

Zinsser, William. *On Writing Well*, Fourth Edition. New York: Harper Perennial, 1990.

Printed in the United States
222081BV00001B/5/P